OOPS

Goofs, Surprises, Errors & Mistakes

John Florian

authorHOUSE®

AuthorHouse™
1663 Liberty Drive
Bloomington, IN 47403
www.authorhouse.com
Phone: 1 (800) 839-8640

Published by AuthorHouse 11/05/2018

ISBN: 978-1-5462-6419-4 (sc)
ISBN: 978-1-5462-6418-7 (e)

Print information available on the last page.

This book is printed on acid-free paper.

PREFACE

I am using an old cliché' to say: "life has many surprises". Among many pleasant experiences there could be as many not so good ones. As some are shocking as well some could be hilarious. I had a life time of those experiences and as I recall them from my memories. I have collected for my readers to share those and make you think or perhaps laugh with me. The collection of this experiences only the most memorable ones which has made the list. It is truly a life time collection, which I encountered from my early employments and from my independent consultation periods. It represents 30 years from the 1960s to the 1990s.Thesewritings consist of a series of short stories, all independent from each other.

You don't have to be familiar with the specific manufacturing methods it will be easy to follow the explanations, and you can understand the outcomes. Some are serious situations; some are costly while others are hilariously funny. What was the challenges I had to face and how to overcome them. Most of the miss haps are the results of bad planning or perhaps results of rushed decision or complete ignorance and maybe plane stupidity, but they are definite "screw-ups"

With the grace of God's help I witnessed, endured, and survived all this situations.

On the other hand you may not found some of the situations interesting and educational, or matching to your taste, but at least I have entertained you.

Just bear with me and learn or even laugh with me.

Thank you for taking the time out to read this writing.

CONTENTS

A vanishing good idea

One day I came up with a good idea. This is the times when the film type of photography was the predominant method to preserve pictures.

The higher quality cameras used a roll type of films which allowed taking pictures repeatedly instead loading and reloading films for each picture. The roll of film is placed into a magazine at the factory and that is how you would purchase it. The magazine with the roll of film loaded into the camera and the leading edge of the film is secured in to the camera's other spool. The camera back is closed and ready to take pictures. After a picture is taken a handle has to be move to crank another film frame ready for the next exposure. When you take a photograph often you realize that the next moment comes a better opportunity to make a better picture. By the time you have wined the film to the next picture the moment to improve the picture is disappeared. There must be a faster way to advance the film to the next exposure.

The idea I came up with is to make the film advancement with a mechanically motorized system which would be part of the camera. After the previous picture, when you release the exposure button, it would automatically trigger the film advancement. In order to have the power to move the film advancement I would employ an ordinary coil spring mechanism. This devise built in to the magazine side of the spool.

After the film loading the film should be wined to the other spool and with that the coil spring is wound tight, fully energized. This energy would be used to advance the film for the next picture. Of course the film is pulled back into the magazine, and at the end all the film will be back in the magazine. The only difference will be that the first picture will be the last picture count.

This way no need for electrical motor and battery power to implement this film advancing task.

The idea looked so promising that I hired a person to write up this proposal to be efficient for a presentation to a commercial company. I made the illustration of the concept. After several months I have chosen one of the largest well known U.S. Company cameras and film manufacture to submit my idea.

Several months later I have received a letter from them. The company's representative stated that my proposal not new at all movie cameras has automatic film advancements, and for still cameras it is not commercially feasible, there for they are not interested in my proposed idea.

Well the good idea went out the door!

But two years lather the Company introduced a brand new still camera with electric drive system with a battery pack. After all the basic idea was good, but not my concept.

Oh well, it is no longer important, because in today's photography no more film used since all picture taking went to digital format which is much improvement over the old system, and the firm is no longer a main provider in this field.

THE ENGINE DROPPED OUT

I had purchased a used car from a private party to provide transportation to work and back home. The car was a

1960 model of a Chevrolet brand. The car was a Corvair model a rear engine job. The motor was in the back end of the car occupying the trunk area while the actual trunk space was in the front.

My wife had the same model car, hers was a two door, and mine was a four door model. We both liked these cars, not too big and not too small.

As I mentioned earlier I purchased this automobile used and it was running satisfactorily. It started fine and moved well in low and high speed. Lots of people and organizations blamed that this car being unsafe and wanted to eliminate its manufacturing. I totally disagreed with these conclusions.

The only thing I had noticed that the engine seal in the back had a small gap in the back side. I thought that someone worked on the motor and did not fit it back correctly, where it's needed to be.

One Monday morning I was heading to work early in the morning. The weather was perfect, bright sun shine and I was feeling good. I left my house with an upbeat feeling, looking forward to my work. As I traveled thru the city on various streets I came up on a major intersection crossing boulevards'. On that intersection was some work done, because when finished they have left a big hump of black tar finish like a speed-bump, hopping that the cars will level it off.

By the time I had recognized it I was on it with full speed. The cross bump pushed the car up and when the rear wheels landed down, I heard a big crunch. The car became very light, the accelerator did not respond, but the breaks functioned. I had enough rolling movement that I could move to the side curb.

Looking back I saw my engine dropped out left on the intersection. I exited the vehicle and went back to see, the motor was still running on the reserve fuel from the carburetor, but ready to stall any moments.

Now what to do?

I went to the nearest phone booth and called my work to tell them that I will be late because the engine dropped out of my car. They told me that I should come up with a better excuse.

Then I telephoned the towing company and when I told them what was my predicament.

After a few moments I told them that mined as well they should pick up the engine in the intersection also.

I could not get more words out, all I heard: Ha-Ha-Ha-Ha

This was the first request for them, and also for me.

Only the motor dropped out, leaving the transaxle with the car so the four wheels remained in the car, therefore I could roll to the side.

The tow service picked up everything and the repair shop fixed the car. After paying a large bill I was happily drown this automobile for a few more years.

FAT TOOTHPASTE TUBES

I worked for a large drug and chemical company in the research laboratory. My duties were to test product stability and long term shelf life expectancy.

One day we have received several boxes of toothpaste products from the company's warehouse. After examination we have found that the toothpaste tubes are extremely expanded, almost touching the carton's sides which they were packed into. Some of the tubes almost compromised the crimped ends which started to unravel. When the cap closure was removed the toothpaste just oozed out like it was under pressure. If you would take a "fat" tube and punctured it with a needle you could hear a hissing noise of the escaping gas. If you aimed the escaping gas to a flame source like a Busan burner the escaping gas would light up, creating a torch like flame about 10 inches long. Of course when the gas escape went down the flame also ceased.

The following conclusion we came up with. At the time the toothpaste formulation made it contained a small amount of chloroform, put in the formula, to give some bite in the mouth as a flavor enhancement. Such formulation was made in all the competing brands at that time period.

In storage at the warehouse the chloroform reacted and was hydrolyzed by the water in the toothpaste and created a small amount of HCl "hydrochloric acid". This acid reacted with the inner surface of the aluminum tubes creating another reactions, producing AlCl "aluminum chloride" and Hydrogen gas which was the source of the flame.

The aluminum tubes should have been lined with wax, which would eliminate the chemical reaction. By ignorantly placing the toothpaste in an unlined aluminum tubes created a disaster. The whole warehouse filled with toothpaste had to be destroyed, not only the toothpaste itself but all the packaging materials as well. It was a complete loss. This is happened just because someone ether ignored the recommendation to use wax lined tubes or forget to put into the production plan, or did not know any better.

This loss was horrendous when a whole warehouse of product had to be destroyed.

Just like frosting on a cake

For this incident I have to go back to the late 1960's. I have worked in the packaging department for a large company's research department. My boss was the director of the entire packaging department.

One day he has come to me with a new innovation which he got from somewhere else outside the company. The idea behind this product was to make premeasured liquid dispensing. There was an insert like a small well which fit into a plastic bottle's neck. It was equipped with a dip tube going down to the bottle's bottom. When the bottle is squeezed the liquid is pushed thru the dip tube and fill the well in the neck of the bottle. When the well was filled the squeezing should be stopped and there was a premeasured amount of liquid is trapped in the well.

The idea was very good, however the physical size of this insert was smaller than any of the plastic bottles we had on hand. We could not find any existing bottles which would fit snugly with the well insert.

My boss told me that just put a few wraps of electrical tape around the well insert that would make and fit snugly. I tried to convince him that method would not make snug enough, and the liquid may lubricate the electrical tape and it would not hold up. He told me, just do it! So I did.

Next I see him in the middle of the room surrounded by company executives and he is ready to demonstrate this new innovation. The bottle is filled a very viscous liquid like {Pepto Bismo} . He lifted in his hand the bottle high so everyone can see and started to squeeze. I could see that he has to squeeze hard enough to force the thick liquid thru the dip tube to fill the well cavity. I have seen his thumb turning white to increase the squeezing pressure.

The next moment the electrical tape gave up, and the well insert popped out. A large globe of liquid exited the bottle up into the air, and the next moment it landed on his bald head. His head was completely covered by the thick pink colored liquid. The liquid runs down on his forehead, covering his eyebrows, and running over the eyelashes. As he blinked the individual eyelash formed a thin string like run off with larger droplets at the end of it just dangling there.

His head looked to me just like a freshly frosted cake. It was hilarious and everybody broken out in a loud laughter, including me. I handed him a towel to wipe off the stuff, however he actually needed a lot more, like a shower.

Each time I bring up this story and the picture come to me I break out in a chuckle, because I vividly see his bald head covered with the pink colored liquid dripping off his eyelash .

To end this story I did not worked for him very long afterward.

First impression of a new job

At this time I am in a new job. My assignments were to develop new products for the company and calling on prospective customers. Just to find out what they want or they needs are and design products we could make out of our material and production techniques. Among visiting the various customers I went to a large ice cream maker who had many franchise ice cream stores under their name. They had been very well known with the multitude of ice cream flavor offering. My appointment was with the department head of packaging of the various ice cream products which was mostly for customers who needed single serving items.

As I was ushered into his office the first thing he told me that his company is in the process of suing my company for various reasons. The only motive he has to accepting my appointment because I was brand new to my company and wanted to test me.

I know right away that I am in a very particular position and I wanted to remedy everything, but it was not going to be easy to climb out of this situation. In the past I have managed to overcome most of the negative predicaments and proved to both sides that everything can be worked out.

However I was upset with my own company that they have not indicated prior to my appointment this negative feeling between the two companies. I felt it was wrong to set me up such a way and at least it should be mentioned to me before. The answer was they also wanted to test me; Baloney!

In time I managed to overcome the negative feelings among our companies and put thru many innovative design ideas to this company. One of my designs received a packaging award from a prestigious packaging magazine. When I have got the recognition award I relinquished it and passed it on to my direct contact of the director of packaging at the ice cream company. I was sure he could benefit his position better with his company then I gain.

After that time we introduced many more new products for his firm. One of the designs I made became so successful that it had a least 20 years of marketing expectancy nationwide. I also learned that many of the competing companies tried to take over the production of that design without any luck. It actually outlasted my employment with my own company.

Sign or don't sign it

Just before I had left the previous company, I worked on an idea which looked very promising. Matter-of- fact it looked so good that we though it could be patented. The company's patent lawyers get involved with the project. I gave them a detailed illustration how it is working.

Then I departed from the company for a better job with higher compensations. I was with my new company for a while and I had received a phone call from the previous company's patent attorney. He was telling me that they have prepared a patent application and they are ready to file it to the government's patent office. And they need my signature as an inventor. He also told me that I am a co-inventor in this application. In *the* invention application my former boss the department supervisor happened to be my co-inventor.

I don't know how he managed to squeeze himself into this position when he never was involved with the project, the only thing he did is supervised the department. Now because he was the boss of mine he made himself a co-inventor?

My first reaction was appealing and turned my stomach, He was not involved with this project in the beginning thru the end and now he is a co-inventor? The only think I could think of he is looking for a carrier advancement opportunity.

At that moment I made the decision not to sign and share the invention with him. He can't force me I am not working for him anymore. That is my final decision.

The patent lawyer explained to me that if I don't sign it he will end up and he will come the sole inventor and he already signed the document. He has convinced me to sign it this way my name will appear as a co-inventor. So I signed it, I had no choice but sharing the glory as a co-inventor. I am also positive that my former boss he did not invented anything else.

At least for me this was my first U.S. Patent.

After all in the later years I have managed to obtain over 19 U.S.Patents as a sole inventor.

Lost and Found

The company I worked for was a primary producer of containers for the food industry. To manufacture this type of tray products it was necessary to make our own plastic sheet stock. When the company purchased the equipment to make the sheet stock they had chosen over sized machinery in order to cover future growth. In the mean time we could produce a lot more than our actual need was to make the food tray products. The excess sheet material we decided to offer for sale. This not only removed the extra sheet stock but we made money, even if this sale was going to our competitions. The extra money was most welcome and it increased our profit margins of ours. Such marketing went on very well for many years, matte- of- fact we have shipped nationwide. Orders came in such large quantities that we shipped by railcars. We had a rail spur next to our plant, which made it convenient. Our shipping department used it frequently to load the sheet stock and sent the railcar to the customers. When the loading was completed the doors where sealed and the railroad company picked it up and delivered it to the destination. However at this time several weeks later we received notification from the railroad company that they experienced a major derailment. They at that time did not know if any damage occurred, but their insurance will cover our losses. It satisfied our company and we made arrangements to reship the lost order.

Behold about a year later we experienced a major break down at our plastic sheet making equipment. The repair and obtainment of replacement of parts was estimated would take longer than a month or maybe longer. This breakdown not only affected any outside plastic sheet sales but directly halted our own food tray production. The biggest fear happened to be unable to produce tray products for our long time customers and could force them to seek product somewhere else, resulting in a permanent loss of business. We worried that they end up with our competitions.

In our desperate situation we had to seek and purchase plastic sheet in the open market to maintain our tray production lines. After many urgent phone calls were made and we had almost given up we found an unknown source that had what we needed. They had railcar quantity plastic sheet goods on large roll stock .The only catch was the price, which was three times over the going price of similar quality of plastic sheets what is the standard market price in the industry. We had no choice but agree to buy the material at the extra ordinarily high price. This way we could meet our obligations to our customers and furnish the tray products what they have ordered.

When this expensive sheet materials arrived to our loading ducts we discovered that the sheet material was the same thing what we had shipped earlier and had gone thru the derailment and been salvaged. The salvage company or its investors sat on this plastic sheet supply waiting for an opportunity to sell at inflated price.

It happened to be exactly us!

NEW CAR SMELL VS A STINKY CIGAR

I just purchased my first new car. It was a VW bus type of a vehicle. Nice red colored with a white roof, which had a sunroof on the top. I used this car to commute from home to work and back. I also used it to transport kids of the soccer team which I was coaching. I could pack the team in and after the games transport them to a quick snack in a fast food place.

I was very proud of my brand new car and enjoyed the clean interior with the cherished new car smell.

At the work place where all the executives parked I parked among them. All the management people had big and expensive cars, except mine a VW next to them.

One day the general manager came to me and asked if I would drive him to his dealership where they serviced his car. I was more than willing to drive him to the car service department. I loved this guy very much, he was always very kind to me matter- of- fact he was the one who hired me and offered a job without a resume, just a good recommendations. I told him that after work we will meet at the parking lot and I will drive him there.

After 5 o'clock we met at the parking lot and I opened the door for him so he could climb in. We saddled in and I started to dive out of the parking lot. He has given me the direction to which way to go and fined the particular dealership.

As we moving on to the freeway he had reached in to his jacket inner pocket and pulled out a huge cigar. I did not liked that at all. The cigar fumes will take over permanently my new car odor and I will have to smell that for a long time after. I was thinking how to avoid this situation without hearting his feelings, and just gently not harshly communicate to him that no smoking allowed in my vehicle.

Quickly I came up with the following: " I don't mind if you light up that cigar, but you have to stand up and smoke that way". I opened the sunroof and if he would stand up his head will stick out over the roof.

He got my signal and put away the big cigar without lighting it. I don't care how stinky he makes his car, but definitely can't do that to mine. I was happy that this incident was resolved.

As we traveling further he has asked me that where my cruise control is. I pointed to my right leg which is pressing the accelerator pedal that is my cruise control. I guess he never driven or traveled in a stick shift car, but find my driving so smoot that it matched his luxury automatic shift car.

After all I had enjoyed the new car smell for a lot longer periods.

No free lunch

The company I worked for was located way out of town. The location was so remote that there was nothing close, only farm fields surrounding the factory. For manufacturing it was ok, for shipping the trucks could easily come and go, and we had our own railroad spur.

The only problem was that there was no food source nearby. All the restaurants and coffee shops were quite a distances away. To feed the employees they have to bring they own lunch with them. The factory workers were used to that arrangement. The executives however did not fit into that category. They like to go out for lunch either as a group or by them self. This situation always took extra time away from their desks and duties.

The owners of the company came up with an idea and solutions. They have decided to hire a cook and set up a kitchen with a room dedicated for lunch. The cook will prepare lunch which will be served to the executive management group. They set up a time twelve noon and the cook would serve lunch which was prepared like a home cooked meal five days a week. By one o'clock all management personal should be back to work at the office. The owners decided who would qualify for the free lunch. No plant workers or the foreman would be invited.

This company was a privately owned company and almost all the executives where either relatives or at least close friends. Only two of us were outsiders from the close knit group. My position with the company was manager of new products and product design. The cut off of acceptance to the free lunch was closed down front of me. That meant that I still have to bring my own lunch from home every day.

I was disappointed, but I had to accept the ruling of the owners. Anyway my lunch from home was not bad at all.

One day an idea popped into my head. I will make a great disappointment and a big joke on the privileged executives. The opportunity came very soon, when one day the cook did not come to work. I did not know the reasons as why the cook did not show up, but I know it when the cook's car was not parked at the designated area. The kitchen lights where off and no activity was in the kitchen.

From my previous job I had several cans of experimental room deodorant sprays. Among them was a can labeled "Danish bakery" smelling like the real stuff.

About 11 o'clock before lunch time I sprayed a big blast of spray into the intake of the air condition, which happened to be in my office. The air conditioner distributed the wonderful smell all over the offices. Nobody could deny that something good made for lunch. At noon all the selected people filed in to the lunch room sat down, fork and knife in hands waiting to be served. When nothing came, one person stood up went to the kitchen found everything cold, but the fresh Danish smell was inviting. Then, several others got up checking if it is true or not, disappointment took over. I do not know what followed this but to satisfy their hunger and the lingering smell, they had to go out for a real Danish lunch.

I did not had the courage to tell anyone that I was responsible for this smell and joke, probably they would kill me and I would smell Danish from underground.

SOMETHING IS FOR YOU, NOTHING FOR ME

I had successfully worked for this company with outstanding customer relations. I had many projects moving forward and I liked my job. The company was also good to us. Once a year they budgeted bonuses for the upper management. This was somewhat of a profit sharing gestures. Late fall was the time to get that bonus. When the time came all the important people received an envelope containing the bonus check. Who got how- much was a secret and nobody reveled the mount a person received.

The firm was privately owned and most of the upper management consisted of relatives or close friends, only two or three of us were outsiders. After all envelops has been distributed, everyone was satisfied. Then they discovered that I was forgotten from the bonus list. No extra money was left in the bonus budget, it was emptied out. It was some embarrassment for management and to remedy the situation they had to come up with a solution. One option they came up is to ask all the recipients of the bonus to give back some money, perhaps $50 dollar per head and that money will cover my bonus allocation.

The accounting department objected to this, because it would not work with the IRS regulations on the reporting of the tax forms may not be acceptable. Anyway the $50 per head was not enough to cover the legitimate size of my bonus. The other suggestion they had is to keep quiet, hopping that I would not notice that I was left out. Actually I was very flustered by the situation after I had invented a new manufacturing method which at that time was experimental, but very promising. The invention was very crucial to our business in that it curtailed to eliminate the sharp edges of the meat trays so it would not cut the wet fingers of the butchers.

I made a decision that if opportunity presented itself I would seek a new Job somewhere else.

At a later time visited the plant and I have saw, that the invention of mine was duplicated on all of the production machines. After all I did a good job in spite of not getting a bonus.

AGGRAVATION IN JOB SEEKING

After being disappointed in the position I had, I was seeking a new one in the same field of expertize. I saw many advertisements in many newspapers and trade magazines. Most of them did not fit me; however one of them caught my interest. It was close to my field of expertize and not too far from my home and I though my qualifications could get that job for me. I prepared a resume and called the company for an appointment. The appointment was set up and I went there on time.

When I showed up I noticed that I was not the only one, instead a large group of applicants were there. They took my name and I should seat and wait when they will call me. After a period of time, finally my name was called. I was ushered into a very tiny room with a chair and a small table. On the table there was a preprinted form and an ordinary kitchen timer. The lady who brought me there set the timer for 1.5 hour and said I should fill out the form on the table. The preprinted form had noting than questions and after each question two boxes to be filled with your agreement or disagreement. None of the questions was work related all was psychological test related questions. I don't remember all the questions; however one still edged into my mind. This question was checking your relations with your mother. The same question has been repeated several times throughout the form, but worded differently. It did not take me very long to figure out this test was nothing but a psychological evaluation to test the individual applicant for their stability.

I was aggravated for much reason. First of all this test should not be the first evaluation. It told me that this company's first priority was not technical knowledge, but something else. Furthermore irritation I had is the ticking kitchen's timer, plus the lack of air in the small closet size room I was placed. I just unfolded the questioner sheet, which contained several folds, and found in the back connecting lines for aiding the examiner for the correct answers, as how accurately was given by the test subject.

I found myself so aggravated and discussed I just stood up opened the door, folded the questioner up to its original form and exited the tiny room. I told the attending lady that I am totally uninterested to obtain employment with this company. I told her that they should hire those individuals who are seated on the bench, and ready to fill the psychology questioner, than just walked out from the promises.

About a year later I found out that particular company had folded, went out of business and their president had resigned. I had a previous run in with that person in another situation and I never was impressed with him. Good thing I walked out and I did not regret that I did not get a job there.

New job jitters

The company who hired me out from my existing job received an excellent recommendation from our shared mold maker. They were most anxious to obtain my services because just recently lost the person who held that position due to unexpected illness. The company was a western regional manufacturing division of a subsidiary of very large oil company.

They had several manufacturing plants all over the country. They covered the entire US with regional products. The plant manager believed that to obtain growth it must be accomplished by introduction of new products. By Introducing a variety of product offering they would secure future growth for the western region. When they heard of me and received good recommendations they contacted me via telephone.

The next step was to get together and meet in person. We met in a restaurant and discussed details of the job. They were offering and if both sides find it mutually satisfactory I could sign up for the new position. They had not invited me to the factory because we had been in direct competition and in case I did not accept a position with them I could carry sensitive information's back to my existing plant. The salary offer was substantially larger than what I received at my old position and they even offered me to pay the relocation expenses.

My fairly new car had given me trouble for over six month; It had a problem with the aluminum alloy engine casing. The casing was too soft and the bolts that were held down the cylinder heads came out of the engine block. The dealer tried to fix the problem but it always came back. The only thing I could do is trade it in and got a newer model. I must have the new car in my possession over three month before I signed up for the new job. It had a more powerful engine plus had air conditioning.

When we moved to the location for my new job, the AC came very handy because it was known to be a very hot location. After about three month one Sunday coming home from church, I saw my old car parked about two houses over my home. It is remarkable that the car was sold about 150 miles away from where I trade it in. I never saw it again I guessed they had found out what was wrong with it.

It took me more than three months to settle down in my new job and learn the large corporation's mentality. It is spectacularly different than a small company. The best way I can described it is like a large battle ship verses a small boat. When the water gets disturbed the small boat can change direction without any hesitation while the big boat did not even feel the disturbed conditions. The same way to reactions for marketing conditions the big corporation go by preset budgets and do not give into any fluctuation in the market place. I just had to reeducate myself and go with the flow, what was a good move in a small company it could be a lesser advantages at the large corporate.

About a month later the plant's manager came to me and told me that the regional manager {big boss} was coming to visit our plant. He wanted me to go and pick him up at the airport, this way I will have a chance to meet him the first time without all the other people's interruption. This way I will have a chance to meet with him one on one . As he left the airplane we exchanged greeting each other and he told me that he was briefed well about my credentials.

As we approached my car he admired it, and as we climbed in to it the first thing he has asked me: "Did you buy this car because of your new job?" and he shook his head. I told him: not so, I need it because my old car broke down. After that no other remark has been said, but this question of his lingered on with me for a long period of time thinking how secure is my position with this company and in his eyes? Maybe he did not think that they need my knowledge and services. I worked for that company for 5 years and introduced many new products for manufacturing, and top on this I have obtained 18 US patents for the company. In the five years of my employment I came on to many situations which I will address in the next few titles.

WHAT BUDGET?

The big corporations operate with the budgeting system. It is like the back bone of the operation, everything is depending on this and if it is approved or disapproved meant to go or not going forward. The various departments submits applications for their projects and the headquarters checks it out and may approve it or deny it. If the requested funds are approved the project could go forward of course the spending had to be watched for not over spending. This budget system makes all operations functional. The application to the corporate headquarter is called AFE which means Application For Expenditure, send in for approval. There are some guess work involves in this and lots of unknown particulars. Even before my hire the company's plant management had to submit a budget application for covering all, my job and the necessary expenses with it. It was not easy because there was some unknown factors involved.

Even before my hire the plant manager had to guess as how much this figure should be. I learned after I moved in my position a month later how much budget allocated for my future efforts. I learned that I can spend no more but if I spend less the following year my budget will be matched to the lesser spending number. This budget would cover all expenses, my salary and my assistant salary plus all travel expenses and any of the test molds we made. I could make as many test molds the budget permits, however I don't have a machine to put it on. In case I choose to put those experimental molds on existing production machines I will be charged time for interrupting the regular production. This can hurt the production schedule and I will run out of my budget. With this curtailment I had to minimize the number of experimental mold making and made only the necessary and the most promising experimental designs.

With these limitations the first year I made only several experimental molds because no equipment was available to experiment, other molds has been sat a side for next year and any unused budget went away. The following second year I had a budget for equipment to purchase, but no budget for molds. It actually took to the third year when the budget dilemma was resolved. We had a machine and molds to put on and could experiment with new product ideas. We set up a pattern making shop, purchased equipment and I got everything I needed.

When we made a successful new product idea and had tested it out a production mold was purchased, then the manufacturing department took it over and we no longer had any responsibility and control. Some time it was difficult to give up control over the projects when we felt like we would giving away our "baby" for which we worked on so hard for. We did not trust the production people to make the best choices for the production of the product idea. Often we had seen that they have used lesser quality of raw materials to produce the items for the market and could have jeopardize the reactions to the new product idea with the costumers.

Some of the new product ideas went very well and we even patented some of the designs for future protections. But it took three years to function correctly because of the budget dilemma.

Combination mold structures "gang molds"

In the production of meat tray products many different sizes of trays are produced. The tray sizes are determent buy the butchers and the size of the cut of meat to be packed into the trays. For example a "New York" steak will require a small size tray, on the other hand a "rib eye" steak need a larger sized tray. Both cut of meat have the same length but different width, so the trays made to accommodate each sizes of meat cut. Of course there are all kind of sizes of meat cuts and there are many sizes of trays were made to accommodate them. The plants engineer who purchased the mold figured out that there are two of the trays the same length. Therefore, he could combine both sizes of tray configurations in to the same mold. This way he could save money, by purchasing one mold instead two. That sounded good and prudent. This way they can manufacture two sizes of meat trays at the same time. Such combination molds do not work with all the sizes but in this case it lends its self to produce meat trays that way. The two particular meat trays allowed doing this, because the trays had common dimeson on one side.

The mold had been ordered and it had the combination cavities placed in to the same mold bed. After running production on the two type of trays it was discovered that while making sufficient quantity of one of the trays the other trays are well over produced. The extra trays were placed into the warehouse. The other thing were also learned that one of the tray which was produced happened to be more popular, than the other trays. In given time the over produced trays quantity get so large it was bulging out of the warehouse. The sales department came to help out and this overproduced trays offered at a reduced price, just to get rid of it. That really did not worked, customers did not buy the over produced trays, just because the price was lower.

Actually the people who were involved, should have investigated prior to the mold purchasing, as how many of the particular cuts of meat slices can be cut from a beef carcass .They would have learned that a beef carcass only produce so many slices of cuts from it and not that many slices of the other cuts.

Advance planning and research is most important to know the market and demand. The marketing department and the butchers input is crucial to know how many trays are used for each cut of meat. A cost saving idea could back fire and cost more in the long run, like In this case. To properly fill the production need it will take two new molds to accomplish this. A lesson is learned, and in order to fix the mold problem two new mold had to be ordered, this way scheduling each production runs for the specific sizes of trays can be controlled.

The combination molds future can be summed up to be discarded or thrown in to a lake and used as a boat anchor, just because of the mold's heavyweight and useless features.

How to kill a new product idea

One of mine new product is aimed to enter into the strawberry marketing. I had designed for this field a most successful product idea before, however it was made out of clear solid plastic. The clear plastic strawberry baskets I had designed in the 1960"s which is still produced today. I had learned that the old type of plastic baskets tend to damage a high number of berries do to the sharp edges of its ribbed design. That is what we solved with the clear plastic baskets. The only problem we had to solve was placing enough holes in the basket to provide ventilation to the fruit to cool it. Way back in time the original wooden baskets had no holes at all, but that was the only available packaging material for strawberries.

Now I was working with a company who makes plastic foam material trays. How can I use this material to make a feasible strawberry baskets. The foam material is soft and less damaging surface to the strawberries, so it could work very well. The only problem I had is how to place vent holes in the foam baskets. Punching holes in the baskets must be done in a secondary step and removal of the punched out pieces is difficult. This secondary operation was also very costly. And top on this the static charges can keep some of the punched out pieces that adhere to the baskets and difficult to remove.

I had to come up with another method to make vent holes in the strawberry baskets. In order to make holes in the sides of the baskets all I had to do is make slits in the foam sheet before forming the baskets at the proper locations. This was to be done prior to heating the foam sheet. I have known that under the heating conditions the plastic material tend to "run away" from the heat source. Therefore the slits will open up like small holes. After forming, the holes will be located on the sides of the baskets if the slits are made in the right locations. This way we eliminated the problem of hole punching and all the related problems with it. The foam strawberry basket was looking good and we went into production with it. We have produced a large number of them and placed them into boxes ready to be shipped to a strawberry grower. It was spring time early in the season and strawberries get the highest price at that time of the year. Everyone looking for fresh fruit treat.

The grower was anxious to fill orders in spite the berries were not totally ripened yet. Some of the strawberries showed large areas of white spots on the berries which indicated that it was not ripened. Anyway the strawberries was packed and got shipped to the supermarkets . The customers looking at the product very quickly discovered that the fruit is not fully ripened, did not purchased it. They also associated the packaging to the green foam baskets with the unripen fruits, and absolutely refused to buy any of them. The lesser quality of strawberries packed in to our green foam baskets killed the product for us. This eliminated any chances to reviving this product line, and make any further production plans. It was a good idea which went away.

BINDING PLEDGE

The company who employed me was part of a national firm, with several plants located in different regions of the country manufacturing the same product lines. This way they could have coverage for all the regions with the same products. It was the plastic division of a chemical company owned by a gigantic oil firm. After starting my employment I was told that each of the management personal had to comply with a specific rule. The rule was that at the beginning of the calendar year we had to make a commitment for the upcoming year. All of us, including the plant's manager, had to put down our commitments as our goal to accomplish for the coming year. We had to do this in writing and placed it into a sealed envelope which was placed in a safe. By the end of the year the envelops will be opened and we will be judged how close or how far we came to our preplanned commitments. This may affect our future pay increases.

I was on the job for two months at the end of the year, but I also had to comply, just like the rest of the management team. We all had different assignments and different goals to accomplish. So it would take different commitments and all the department supervisors would have to make the pledge to match the positions they are in, weather what is reasonable or not.

For example the operation's manager could have put down that he will minimize the equipment breakdowns. I would not know as how that can be done, because he or she is not in control of that. While the manager of plant safety operations commit to have fewer accidents. The production's manager will state as to how much products will be produced.

This motivation technics sound good at first, but could back fire and very fast run against the intended goals. True the year time many changes could come and make those pre commitments absolute. Market conditions change, new legislations come forward, raw material supply change, major equipment break down, and many more come to life and can throw the "monkey wrench" into the play.

For example loss of business orders would require production to be slowed down, but by the earlier made pledge the production manager has to fill his promise, therefore he will fill the warehouse with unwanted products. The extra products ties up raw material supply and may not allow other products to be made. It Is ties up money and contribute to higher inventory taxes. Markets change and what was a hot item be come a stagnant item, causing unintended consequences.

My personal predicament was somewhat different; as I committed to introduce a given number of new products. The commitment did not specify that the ideas at what stages to be accomplished. Ideas on paper do they have to be actually produced items. I was off the hook, and let someone judge me. On the other hand I was sorry to see the other management personal, especially the production manager who committed to produce an extra volume of products to meet his earlier made commitment. I would recommend that the genius person who invented this motivation technic and management concept causing such a ill effects should be forced to eat the unwanted products.

He or she must have drawn a large salary not only one time but for many years, and if the initiator goes somewhere else they will create the same problem, again and again . There should be other ways to make factory management more productive and the same time life easier.

FACTORY HYGIENE

Working in a plant which produces food grade tray products is an important part of the of knowledge as how food products gets to the consumers. Many of the plastic trays are part of the package which holds the food, making sure that the food remain clean without any contamination. Foods packaged in trays can be shipped, displayed and carried home.

Food packaged into trays whether they are dry or wet, none perishable or fresh with limited shelf life. It is mandatory that the plastic trays are produced in a cleanly manner and transferred in the same way to the packagers without any chance of contamination. All of the food packagers and food handlers are obligated to maintain a food grade clean environment which is overseen by governmental agencies like FDA., USDA. The food safety act is established and strongly enforced in the food handling operations. For example: butchers, meat packers and bakers must wear hair nets and facial protectors if they have facial hair, so no food can be contaminated by fallen hair. This includes food servers as well.

Unfortunately to my entire carrier working in the plastic industry producing trays for food, I had never seen any of food safety protectors used. The general conceptions was that when the plastic trays are made the processing heat will destroy most of the living contamination, therefore it is exempt from those rules. When the trays are made, they Immediately get stacked and packaged into plastic sleeves eliminating any chances from contaminations.

This secondary handling bothered me from the very beginning of my carrier. There are many chances to obtain contaminations at that segment of manufacturing.

One day I was walking on the plant's floor and I walked beside an operating machine which was producing trays for food packaging, specifically for a supermarket meat department. The time was in the early afternoon at shift change time. The new crew came on duty and started the operation. As I walked by the machine's operator jumped on the platform which was used to receive the stacked food trays ready to be pushed into the plastic sleeves. He had no trays coming out yet, but he tried to loosen some jam problem. I was close enough that I could see he had cowboy boots on and between the sole and the hill he had a large clump of horse manure. I guess he attended horses before coming to work. Of course I chased him off the platform and talked with his supervisor, to let him know what had happened. The production went on and no governmental agency was ever involved. To my knowledge as of today there is no regulation covering the tray production segment of this industry, and I wonder how many times such incident happened and is happening right now.

DEMANDED REGULATION

When plastic foam products are made it would require some kind of gasification or blowing agent to produce bubbles in the plastic mass. The blowing agent is usually introduced under pressure into the molten plastic and saturate the entire bulk before it is extruded. There are many kind of blowing agents used, some are made to rapid expansion while others are slow to react to form bubbles. These bubbles are also referred to as cells. The cell structure is an important part of the product and what is the intended use of it. Larger bubble cells create a ridged form of foam while smaller cell structure make the plastic more pliable. The foam manufacturer choose the particular foaming agent to produce the ideal foam structure for they product line.

In this case the products were made for a tray type of items and were made with uniform foam structures. The particular blowing agent was picked to produce a semi flexible tray product. The specific blowing agent was a type of gas which has been chosen form several blowing agent, introduced under high pressure into the extruder. The extruder blends the blowing agent with the molten plastic resin uniformly, and when this exits the extruder It will have ideal foam structures. Each bubble contains the blowing agent gas, and that is how it is made.

The particular gas is judged as an air pollution agent and the air pollution district and EPA wanted to eliminate it entering it to the atmosphere. I myself do not know which agency was involved, but they have made a demand to place several expansive gas trapping devises onto the roof. Each containing charcoal filters to trap the escaping gas from the air. The company had no choice just spend the money and install the demanded equipment. On top on this, they had to make periodic filter changes and make proper disposal of the filter media.

The very fact of this scenario is that this particular gas is heavier than the ambient air and will remain on the floor and escape through the open doors. It has very little chance to reach the ceiling and get captured in the filter units, unless by a remote occasion a rear draft will carry it up there. At the introduction of the blowing agent there should not have an escape of gas, and what is inside the bubbles of the plastic foam is actually trapped inside for limited time. The rolls of foam sheet are transported outside after is made to let the trapped gas to migrate out of the cell structures and let the air replace it. The trapped gas still goes to the atmosphere, but not inside the plant, therefore the demanded filter system proved to be useless, but money had to be spend to satisfy the demand.

UNCONTROLLED CONTROLLER

There are many responsibilities to operate a factory and all the responsibilities cannot be handled by one person. The entire operation is headed by the plant's manager or operation manager, who has a staff of people under him. This staff is important to the successful operation and carries many discipline area. All of the staff members report to the plant's manager and usually cover the reporting in a staff meeting which is held periodically. This staff could be several people who cover a large discipline area to cover the entire operations. Under the plant manager's wing is the plant's engineer who has the responsibility to cover the building and all the supporting equipment in the building. There is the production manager who is in charge of the production equipment and maintenance department. After that there is the personal department manager who handles the factory staffing, and the manager of the shipping department is part of the staff. We cannot exclude the quality control and the accounts payable department. But most of all is the plant's controller who controls all the money situations. He is the most important department head; he sees all the budget allocations and adherence to it. He handles all the expense's including all the travel expenses the staff inquires. Normally when someone travels we carry our own expenses on our personal credit cards and send it to the controller for reimbursement.

This way he can see if it fits the budget criteria and it is a permissible expense.

It is funny that when you travel and in your expense report you state that you had a couple beers at the airport it is not justifiable, however if you state that you had a couple "refreshment" it is acceptable.

To finish with the story, the controller was traveling to a meeting for business reasons to attend a meeting for controllers out of town. The office received a collect call from the controller that he has arrived at the city of his destination and he is at the car rental booth but the car rental agency would not accept his credit cards because all of them are maxed out. He has no way to rent a car or furthermore pay for the hotel accommodations. He definitely needed help with this predicament. How a controller can be trusted with the company's finances when he is out of control of his own.

A QUALITY CONTROL ERROR

The company manufactured plastic disposable cups. To customize the cups they were printed with the customer's logo. The customer provided the art work for the logo and the message plus the color they wanted to have on the cups. First the plastic cups are made, than the cups receive the appropriate printing. When the cups are produced they are inspected by the quality control {QC} inspector than transferred to the printing department. The printing department has received the complete art work for the label. The QC inspector has a complete run sheet following the order which has all the specifications of color matching. Of course the specifications has the size of the order to state the number of cups to be made. The printing department usually draws from stock a little more to cover any errors in the printing procedure. The QC manager pulls the printing order and secures the appropriate ink colors for the job. As the printing begins the QC inspector checks the print job and makes a color match before further printing is approved. When the printing ink is cured one more check is made, because at drying sometime color change can happen. When everything is acceptable the cups are stacked and put into plastic sleeves, placed into boxes, and the numbers matched to the order size. It is ready to be ship.

In this particular shipment the QC department approved the printing job matching the final details: the logo is OK, the color matching the color chips, and the quality of printing was satisfactory. The order was ready to be shipped and this order came in from Hawaii and it was loaded in to an overseas container. The shipment left the factory. Several weeks later the company received a phone call from Hawaii the order arrived, but the cups has the wrong printing job, The logos on the cups is somebody's else logo and not the companies who made the order. The manufacturer's sales department went into high gear to find a specific food company whose name was on the logo.

Unfortunately there is none in Hawaii with that name, and the cup became useless. At this point the company had two options to rescue the situation. One is to ship the cups back to the mainland, which proved to be more expensive than the cups worth. Secondly the cups can be destroyed. This is exactly what the company has chosen, to take the cups to the land fill. To making sure that this was done right.

They sent the director of the QC department to Hawaii to supervise the destruction, making sure that the bulldozer runs over the boxes of the cups and with than the destruction were made complete.

The head of the QC department used this opportunity to make a vacation out of the trip and took his wife with him to Hawaii.

Premature celebration

I was summoned to Minnesota help to speed up production of video cassettes cases. The manufacturer had a problem; the machine cycled too slow to meet the deadline to produce a large quantity of video cassette cases. I did not know the details of the agreement between the buyer and the manufacturer. They may have had a certain delivery schedule and which involved penalties for late delivery. All we had known that with the current cycle time the product will not make the delivery schedule. The machine was operational and everything on it was functioning, just too slow. I have worked with the machine's operator closely and he followed my recommendations precisely. The major difficulty was to tune the heating cycle to the to the mold movements and the cooling times. If any of this was out of kilter, the product was not made satisfactorily. Not enough heat rendered poor details in the plastic forming and any of the increased heat levels could produce deformed products. Everything must be timed precisely to function properly. If we change one factor it will affect the other conditions. It actually required precise tuning all the manufacturing conditions.

It took time and effort to obtain the ultimate settings. We carefully made the adjustments, but in the mean time we produced unusable products. Finally we reached our goal and the ideal speed of production. With several hours behind us we finally reached the cycle time we wanted.

At that point I looked up to the upper floors where the sales department offices were located. All the sales people were leaning on the hand rails, some of them had stop watches in their hands and checking the speed results. When they confirmed the cycle time was correct they went back to the office and brought out of bottles of liquor and poured it into glasses to celebrate. As the celebrations continued the alcohol made them satisfied. This made them happy that the order will be completed on time. We all could see the satisfaction on their faces, and the glow in their eyes.

As the celebration went on at that moment the machine ran out of the plastic sheet supply and operator had to shut down. He went to the stockroom to get a new roll of plastic sheet which is a six foot roll. It took him to find a roll for this specific product line. It took 20 minutes to bring it to the floor with a forklift. We had just lost 20 minutes of production time and top on this the new material from an unheated storage was way too cold. To bring the material to the same temperature probably will take a day or more. If we increase the heat levels to compensate to the lower heat levels all the other setting have to be changed again, and that will take time. The operator should have staged the new material earlier. All our earlier efforts went out the window and the sales department should have poured back the left over drinks into the bottles. The only accomplishment I done is to prove that to increase cycle time can be accomplished, but without a "Monkey wrench" put into the situation. The early celebration went to hell.

8" C-CLAMP ALMOST
A WIDOW MAKER

In the same state of Minnesota we went to see a factory which at the time was not operating. The location was in a very remote area; mostly farm land surrounded the plant. Since the plant was not operating and no workers was on the floor or cars in the parking lot. We had to travel by car to this location, about one hour or a little more to get there. When we arrived it was almost evening and getting dark. The man who has took me there was the operation manager and he had the keys to the factory.

As we entered the plant none of the lights were on and no windows let lights into the factory's floor. As I could make out on the plant's floor several machines was side by side, all of them shut down. The fellow ushered me to a particular machine's side which he wanted to show me. He had several concerns; however I could not answer him, because the machine was not running.

It is very difficult to make evaluations and give advice when a machine not running. I can't give useful evaluations in this situation and top on this it was very dark. He insisted that I should look into the molding area so I can see it better. He pushed open the safety guard to gain a closer view of the particular area he was concerned with. I leaned in as much as I could, but because it was dark I could not see much. As I leaned in even more in to the machine he tried to open the safety gate further more. As he moved the gate open a large 8 to 10 inch cast iron C clamp dislodged from the top of the safety gate close to 10 feet above. The C clamp dropped down and fell on the floor; it had missed my head but was so close that I could feel the air movement on my face. That is how close it fell from my head. We both turned white but could not tell that in the darkness. We stepped away from the machine, went out of the plant, he locked the door and went back to the car. As we drove back to town neither of us was talking to each other. We both realized how close we came to a serious accident. Injuries can happen very fast and top on this we were great distances a way to get help. When I think of this incident I know now how close I was to make my wife a widow.

Pig roast vs. Truck
bed liner making

For this job I had to travel to Puerto Rico. The company hired me to come and straighten out the manufacturing of truck-bed liners. They produced the truck-bed liners out of thick black plastic sheets. The finished product was stacked and shipped to the mainland, mostly for Toyota pickup trucks. I guessed the reason for having the job here because lower labor cost, in spite of added shipping cost. To reduce the cost of heating the plastic sheets, they chosen natural gas instead of electric power, because the electric energy was a lot higher in Puerto Rico. Gas was more reasonable price wise, and that is why they purchased the equipment with gas heaters.

With gas heaters the entire oven area is equipped with gas jet orifices, approximately about 300 or more. These gas jets should have small enough flames to heat the plastic sheet uniformly.

The first thing I observed was a big flare like flames in the heating chamber. I said to the operation manager: What you trying to do, roast a pig? The problem was that in the past they had a plastic sheet melt down and the molten hot plastic plugged up some of the gas jet orifices. The gas which should go to the plugged orifices exited on the open gas jet orifices making the large flames. This created an uneven heating of the plastic sheet, any area which had no flames was too cold to shape the truck-bed liner and where the flames was big the plastic sheet was way over heated, almost to the point of a meltdown. This could have jeopardized not only the forming of the product but could burn the entire factor down.

The ideal condition would be to have all gas jet orifices clean and even heating throughout the heating chamber. The orifices must be cleaned and the plugged orifices reactivated and it should be part of a repeated maintenance duty.

Roasting a pig should be done somewhere else but not here! The answer to the heating problem was to clean the gas orifices and the problem was solved.

They had other problems, which happened to be in the cooling segment of their production. After forming the truck-bed liners enough residual heat remained in the thick plastic body which needed to be removed. If the truck-bed liner remained hot it will deform easily. That heat must be removed as soon as possible. To cool the formed truck-bed liner the best way with cooling fans. They have known that, they had a problem and the operation manager was dissatisfied with the lack of cooling. So they installed 10 powerful 1Hp fans, five for each side of the truck-bed liner. Soon he had found out that this oversized cooling arrangement still do not do the job. He asked me to evaluate the process and make recommendations how to make improvements.

After a careful study of the procedure I did the following: I took a small paper sheet and tore it to small pieces and placed it in my clutched hand. The paper pieces in my hand moved it to the bottom area of the truck-bed liner and released it. The released paper pieces they did not fly out, just stayed and danced around in the bottom. With this test I proved to myself and the operation manager that there is no cooling air movement getting in to the truck-bed liner. The 10 powerful fans initially blow air in but then create an invisible dome of an air bubble over the entire truck-bed liner surface. No air movement can penetrate it, just like trying to blow air into a bottle. If there is no air escape than there is no air exchange, and no cooling will happen.

So my recommendation was to remove most of the powerful fans and just leave two or three on one side of the truck-bed liner and let the air flow from one side to the other. It will make the air flow better and cooling more viable. They could make it more efficient if the air supply would come in from outside of the plant thru the roof. Outside air is usually a lot cooler than inside the plant environment.

One more change I recommended was that the clamp frame mechanisms should have depressurization escape at least two sides not just one side of the truck-bed liner, so all sides will disengage at the same time, releasing at once this eliminating the distortions on the flanges.

I left and came back home with good feeling that I did my job good and helped the people to manufacture the truck-bed liners better than before.

LANGUAGE PROBLEM

I was in Southern California on behalf of a client trying to produce an experimental new product idea. The client secured time in this plant to use their machinery and make a test run. I was the negotiator for this project. Basically the client paid for the time for which the plant interrupted the production and placed our experimental mold into the machine. The factory allowed us to use the machine and their machine operator who was assigned to the particular machine, whatever I told the operator he should follow my instructions.

First made the setup and placed our experimental mold into the molding machine. Made the setting as close as we could come to. Thinking that when we start molding we could fine tune all those required settings. First we set the temperature criteria, then the mold timing which was the basic setting for the molding.

As the mold closed on the heated plastic almost immediately the air pressure made a hole in the plastic. Conclusion we made that the air pressure was too high. I instructed the operator to reduce the incoming air pressure. The operator climbed under the machinery to make the adjustment. The next molding it was a repeated results to the first experience. We needed to reduce the air pressure again. The operator again went under the machine to reduce the incoming pressure. We went thru this the third time and the fourth time without any satisfactory result. The only thing different was the blow through delayed and happened a little later.

We came to the conclusion that it was something wrong and had to stop the experimentation. We just run out of the time allocations for my client. Removed the experimental mold from the machine and let them go back to their regular production.

I left the promises very disappointed and blamed myself for the failure. As I was driving back home, close to three hours long, I went over in my mind, the situations with fine detail, to come up with an answer. What could have gone wrong and what happened there. At that moment it downed on me: each time I asked the operator to reduce the incoming pressure he went under the machinery to adjust the pressure. But he went to the wrong valve. He adjusted the flow control valve, which did not reduce the pressure only delayed it. He may have misunderstood my instruction or did not know which valves control the pressure.

The machine operator did not speak English well and I could not communicate with him in Spanish. Each time I asked him to reduce the pressure he has adjusted the wrong valve, no wonder the experimentation failed.

The outcome was a failure, not because the experimentation did not work, but possibly a failure of language problem.

I learned something for the future.

MISTAKEN IDENTITY

I was summoned to go to the east coast by my customer to see their operation with one our newly manufactured trays for a frozen cake. The trays were placed under the cake to hold it when it is packaged into a box. The operation was overwhelmingly large and most efficient and everything went very well.

After my visit I had to catch a plane to go back home to the west coast. I checked out of my hotel because it was the right time, I did not wanted to pay for an extra day. I had way too much time before my airplane's departure.

At first I thought would I spend the five hours at the airport, but it was way too much time to spend there.

As I was driving toward the airport on my way I saw a plant on the side of the road with the same company sign I was working for. An idea popped in to my head, I should stop by and visit them. This would help me to kill the extra time I had on my hand. I just pulled in to their driveway and entered the parking lot. To my surprise there was no entrance security, so I could pull up to the building. I entered the lobby and I handed my business car to the receptionist. She took my card and jumped up and run into the offices.

John Florian

The next moment I was ushered in to the offices, where the entire management team lined up in a single row and one by one introduced them self and shook my hand. They were in suits and had neck ties on, like they were expecting someone important. After meeting all of them they took me to the factory floor and showed what is done there.

I was wondering what was going on here, but before I had a chance to come up with an answer they ushered me into the conference room. There was a big table loaded with tempting food set up for sampling and eating. They offered me to seat and help myself to this lavish treats. Now my puzzlement went even higher, trying to figure out as why this was happening, especially for me. I just could not figure it out, so I sampled a few things and I told them that I was not hungry. I was overwhelmed by the hospitality, but I did not think that they did this kind of treatment who ever wonders into the factory. I just do not have an answer, why me?

After my visit I told them that I have to leave and a plane to catch and they have a very nice factory and good management and all of them doing a fine job.

As I left the factory and started to pull out of the parking lot I saw a big limo type of a car pull in the parking lot loaded with several company executives. It just downed on me, this is the people the factory was expecting, and they are the real people who will inspect them. They just made a mistake thinking that I was the official inspector. They thought I was the one, that is why I was treated me well and went out of their way.

Seeing these corporate executives coming in I stepped on the gas and moved out as fast as I could. I do not wanted to be accused of impersonating someone else and perhaps squeezed for the consumed food I taken.

I went to the airport and boarded the airplane and left to the west coast, laughing all the way. Went back over the events and recalling what has happened, it was just a mistaken identity.

What made me laugh even more, and harder when I was thinking that as I left all the plant's staff members high fived each other for a successful plant inspection after all turned out well for them. They have probably pulled their neckties off, and removed their jackets and celebrating, and possibly raided the food stuff on the conference table.

In the next moments learned that the real corporate executive group just showed up at the front lobby door.

SPA SHELL MANUFACTURING

I traveled to Ohio where there was a large national company's manufacturer who was working to make spas. The company was a well -known producer of kitchen and bathroom appliances. This division was making plastic spa shells which put together as complete spas to compliment they product offering. I did not know where the entire assembly was made but I was called in to look at the spa shell forming process.

The spa shells are made out of heavy acrylic sheet stocks which come from an outside source and came in different marbleized patterns and in pastel colors. The colors were in light blue, green, and beige, yellow, brown and of course white. The spa colors were preordered by the customers for the spas. That order sequencing changed from one color to the other without any uniformity.

The reasons they called me in that in was the forming of the spa shells did not get consistently good results. Some of the spa shells were over heated some of them were not formed well, showing to be cold forming temperatures. But, most of the spa shells were satisfactory; they wanted to reduce the number of rejected shells.

The machine operator used a timer {ordinary kitchen timer} to judge the heating time for each spa shell.

After close examination I came up with the following conclusion. It is not proper to timing all the heating cycle the same way. The plastic sheet supply is not the same temperature coming into the operation. The ambient temperature of the warehouse will have seasonal temperature differences and the color of the sheet stock also absorbs the heat input differently. Darker colors heat up faster than lighter ones; actually white color material takes longer to heat up. Since each forming of spa shells made of different colors the heating time should be different. By using the same elapsed time for each forming procedure causes different results.

In order to remedy the situation another method should be employed. My recommendation was to use an "electric eye" system. When the plastic sheet is heated it develops a sag which indicates that the material is heated. The sag size should be the indicator that it is ready to be formed. By positioning an electric eye system to read the sag when the light beam is interrupted would indicate that it is ready to be formed. The height of the electric eye system can be adjusted so in order to make uniform results.

I tried to explain the method to the engineer supervisor but he did not understand the concept. I tried with the help of drawings by detailed explanations with no results. I even spent the time at diner together to convince the fellow to follow my recommendations. No way he could see it and change the system. Because of his lack of understanding the forming procedure remained the same and the number of rejected parts remained the same.

What a waste of my and his time!

THE JUDGE'S DILEMMA

I was summoned to Georgia to a civil litigation as an expert witness. I had to go from the west coast to the east coast for a court case which is a lengthy time to travel plus the 3 hours' time difference. The court house was in Macon, Georgia, that is where the judge will hear the case. At 9 AM they opened the court room and all of us piled in, the attorneys and their assistances and all the people who were involved. It was a large group of people. The two lawyer group taken the position up front, the Plaintiff to the right side while the Defendant to the left side, the rest of us seated in the back. When the judge entered the court room we all stood up. The judge happened to be a large framed man with white hair and a very commending voice, and had a Southern accent, First the two attorney's presented their case and then the judge asked all the expert witnesses to identify their qualifications. When it was my turn I stated that I was a plastic expert and I am knowledgeable of the material and its manufacturing methods. I handed to him my book on the subject. He briefly paged through it and he said that he accepted my qualifications. He screened others after that and some were accepted others been rejected.

When it came to my testimony I stated that since the actual product sample no longer was available {lost in the skirmish of the accident} I cannot positively tell that the product was faulty or its manufacturing had an error. I had tested all the other submitted subsequent samples and all proved to be satisfactory. That was my statement and I stepped down from the witness stand.

As the two opposing attorney arguing they case the judge stops the proceeding and points a finger to me and said: "you come to my chambers" . I am thinking what I have done or why I am picked on, what should I do, I stood up and followed the judge to his chambers and as he entered he took off his black robe and sat down in his big easy chair. He pointed again to me to seat down and said: "I have a dilemma, which of the two F****s is telling the truth."

After hearing this I poised for a few minutes, I was surprised by the judge's blunt, crude but frank language. I told him that he is the judge he has to figure that out.

He told me that the reasons he has asked me because of my fair testimony I sounded most reasonable in this case. After that discussion, I went back to the court room and both attorneys looked very puzzled, what has happened.

The judge dismissed the case as no walled reasons to the argument, period.

JUST MADE ME ILL

I was holding a seminar program in the city of Atlanta. The two days presentation went very well. After closing the program and all the attendants went a way I cleaned up the meeting room and hauled all my demonstration materials back to my room.

I felt tired, but proud of this accomplishment, I needed some relaxations and perhaps some treat. I thought what better way I could do that than going to the top floor of my famous hotel "Peachtree Plaza" which has a bar on top, and it is rotating around. The floor is moving around in such a way that you could see the entire city and its suburbs. When you seating there you don't have to move at all the building's floor will move you around.

So I went there and enjoyed the view and I was resting.

To top off my relaxations I ordered a drink. I told the waitress to bring me the favorite drink of Atlanta in a largest glass with umbrellas and all the works. She did that exactly and I was enjoying it tremendously.

After a little over an hour, turning around and I had seen everything in the city finished my drink I went back to my room and went to bed.

A little later I woke up not feeling good at all. As time went by I started feeling very bad and the feeling got worst. I thought I have food poisoning, I don't know what was in my drink, but sure made me sick. I was very close to call for a doctor. A little later on I started feeling a little better and in the late morning I get up, feeling weak but ready to board my flight to go home.

In another occasion I was in the Southeast of US close to the ocean where seafood was on the main menu. After work I was seating at the counter of an oyster bar. They offered fresh raw oysters with very tasty cracker type bread. The attendant was shocking the oysters, one after the other, and I was eating them as fast. I enjoyed the treat and lost count how many I consumed, maybe a dozen or more. I was full and went back to my room in the same hotel.

In the morning I had to catch a flight home from the east coast to the west. It was a nonstop flight. I got on the plane alright, but when we got airborne the raw oysters in my stomach got they revenge! I had to go to the lavatory in the hurry and take care of an urgent diarrhea problem. I was glued to the toilet just could not get off. I heard the pilot telling the passengers to buckle up we will come to turbulent weather and we will bounce around. I was in the lavatory and just could not leave. There is no seatbelt there and it is located in the back of the plane, where the bouncing is greater. I was holding on to everything I could.

Finally close to our arrival I could leave my prison, feeling better and not thinking of oysters again for the future. How many people can say, I was on the "can" from east to west, but actually I was at this time.

No rooms available

The next three segments are involves traveling. When I was consulting I had to travel extensively, and when had travel there are all kind of misshapes you have to face. When traveling in behalf of a client or holding seminars, particularly for holding the seminars the client makes most of the arrangements for accommodations. Mostly this involved room reservations, meeting room and supplies, including hiring a temporary secretary for my help. I made my own travel plans, which included airline tickets. At end of the seminar I send a bill for my service and all the incurred expenses for reimbursement

This type of an arrangement worked out for many years and all of us involved were satisfied. I have traveled throughout the country, mostly in the industrial hubs. The seminar company organized much different type of seminar programs in various discipline subjects, one of which was mine. They made all the advertisements and collected all the fees from the attendees. I made money for them and I received satisfactory reimbursement for my effort, and the same time I gained future contacts for my consultation business.

For the two day seminar program I had to arrive a day before and leave the location the next day after the program because of my home base location in the west coast. Many programs were scheduled at the east coast location or mid-west. It wasn't hard but not easy ether, usually I left very early in the morning and arrived late in the evening . By the time I arrived to the hotel usually it was at the evening hours.

Several times it happened that when I was ready to check in I was informed that they do not have a room for me. Usually they are over booked or the previous tenant did not checked out as planned and no additional room was available. This presented a problem for me, because the seminar program is scheduled for the next morning in the same hotel's conference room.

The hotel where I was booked most of the time tried to help me out by making arrangement in a nearby hotel. This was not the best situation due to the distance I had to travel there and especially in the morning to come back to the hotel where the seminar was held. In many occasions it would involve a taxi transport. Some times the hotel tried to help me out and set me up with a suite hotel room arrangement which is basically a meeting room and only has a sink and toilet and no bed, but they will provide a temporary cot instead. To sweeten the arrangement and make my disappointment less they will give me reduced charges. This just did not made me feel better at all because the reduced charge benefited my employer while I was receiving a lesser accommodations.

They promised me that next time they will do better. Oh well I was at the short end of the stick. One time in Chicago when I went there they have put me in the far out wing of the high priced hotel, because the hotel was over booked. The outside temperature was -20F and that wing area were not heated. When I went to my room it was freezing cold. The central heating was not on and the only heat source I had is a hairdryer. I filed the bathtub with hot water to heat the room, but it made the area steamy and wet. The marble wall panels and floor started frost up. The bedding had one blanket and the bed spread, good thing I had an overcoat to cover myself, I just made a promise I never going to Chicago in the winter month.

A RISKY SITUATION WITH US CUSTOMS

This time I had to go to Canada, I had been there several times before, specifically in the Toronto area. I collaborated to build a company to manufacture automobile headliners. But this time I was in Montreal working with another company. After finished with my work I was heading home to California. My airplane flight was a direct flight from Montreal to LAX. To my surprise the airport in Montreal had US customs at that location. I don't remember if it was the same in Toronto when I departed from there. Any way it was a total surprise to me especially that it was close to my departure time. As I walked in the custom inspection area I was the only one needed to be inspected. I had two suitcases and the briefcase with me and a carryon cart. The smaller suitcase was filled with my personal clothes while the larger one had plastic samples and many partial aluminum casting for demonstration purposes. The two day meetings always go very well and the attendees liked my presentation, especially the samples which they handled one by one. Now I was ready to go home, and at the airport I had to go to the customs check point. As I approached the examination table the custom officer pointed to the smaller suitcase and asked "what is in it"?. In a very demanding and arrogant voice .I though he was mad at me or maybe got up on the wrong side of the bed.

John Florian

I just ignored his harsh, unfriendly and demanding voice, and answered him that in that suitcase are nothing but my dirty underwear.

He ordered me to open it up, and when I did and he went through it with his gloved hand and then he was satisfied and let me close it back up. After than he placed it to the moving belt which will take it to the airplane loading area. Then he has grabbed my other suitcase and without any hesitation he also placed it on the moving belt, without any question or check. I was so surprised because that suitcase was extremely heavy with the aluminum castings and almost pulled his arms out of the socket. I was holding my breath, as he tagged it as free to go. I was surprised the extra weight did not alert him to check that suitcase, if that would happen and he found the castings suspicious as maybe bomb parts or illegal rocket components he could detained me for a lot longer time questioning . This type of interrogations could have made miss my flight.

Oh, well you can gain or lose in some instances, but at this time I made it back without any problem.

LOSING THE LUGGAGE

When you travel if the airline losing your luggage it is all ways inconvenience, especially when the loss takes place for an outbound trip. If you gone only a few times it is still inconvenient, but when you travel a lot the chances to experience such is happen more often . There was years when I traveled a lot, in a course of a year close to 250 days I was a way.

One time I was heading to Palm Beach, Florida when the airline lost my luggage. The problem was that I arrived the day before my seminar. In my suitcase which did not arrived was my clean close, shaving kit and my slide program. The hotel where I were staying and holding the seminar program was in a very exclusive area. The local ordinance did not permitting to have an in house store facility and no taxi could park there to make pickups. So in order to go to a convenient store to purchase at lease a shaving kit I had to use a limo service. That was the most expensive shaving kit I could buy.

Other time the airline misplaced my luggage with my slide program in it. The first day I had to apologize not to having the slide presentation and had to improvise and using drawings instead. I told the attendees, jokingly that I could make a shadow show with my hands on the screen but it would be irrelevant to the program. One time when the airline did not bring my luggage I was missing things. After the first day I had to ask my temporary secretary to drive me to the airport to pick up my misplaced luggage. When I walked into the baggage claim area there was my suite case on the floor and the two attendants smoking and relaxing without any plans to send me the displaced luggage After all they have made me to sign for it like they did they job well. I was heading to the east coast from the west using a small commuter airline to make connection with a cross country airliner. As we boarded the small aircraft and the same time the attendants loaded the luggage in the back. As we all seated to our assigned seats and the pilot started the engines, the aircraft started to move. True the window I have seen the luggage cart with a few luggage on it and two of mine was there also. They did not load it, because we may reached the load limit of the small airplane. I guess they will forward it with a later flight, there was no flight that day. I know right than that I will have problem lather on. They should have removed me from the aircraft with my luggage all together. I could not stop the aircraft so I left without luggage.

I was going to Ohio, about 100 miles south of Cleveland when the airline did not get my luggage there with me. I registered a claim with the lost luggage department and rented a car and I went to my destination. The luggage was missing and I had to make my presentation in the same clothes I had arrived in. The second day went by the same way, no luggage and after the third day morning I was ready to leave when a taxi showed up with my lost luggage, both suite cases. I did not wanted to open them, was ready to go to the airport. So I told the taxi driver to take me to the airport, this way I did not had to call a cab he was right here. I made my mind up that at the airport I will change to clean close to go home, which was most welcome.

A friend of mine was telling me a story: when I was complaining for frequently lost luggage. They had a fixed reservation, which they could not delay for any reasons: In the Bahamas for a ten days' vacation where they have rented a large sail boat. Two couples together, the husbands are avid sailors and they can handle the big boat with confidents and no fear of the open sea. On they arrival the boat was ready to go, but my friend's luggage did not arrived. When they made the claim for lost luggage they have learned that the next plane will come two days later. They did not wanted to lose the time so they boarded the boat and started they scheduled journey. He has used his travel close to start with and at the open sea he switched to his wife's outfit to walk around the deck. Good thing, they were the same size, and when they came close to another boat he went under into the hull not to be seen in a women's outfit.

I had another experience with lost luggage. I was holding a two day seminar program when both my suite cases did not arrived. The airliner company promised that as soon as they can, will deliver them to me. But they gave some money for spending for most essentials like tooth brush, toothpaste and shaving kits. This was a very nice move for them but it was also a very rear case. I have learned with that many incidents of luggage loss that I packed most of the essentials in to my carry on briefcase, which is not an easy task. Always had a feeling that something I forget.

I was always loaded down when I was traveling for business. I had a brief case, one small suitcase for my close, one large suitcase for my demonstration samples, a suiter to carry my suites, and a luggage cart. I have learned how to stack all this on the cart so I can maneuver in any airport and tight hotel lobby's.

Snow, Snow, and more Snow

I had to go to Wisconsin and my flight was scheduled from Chicago to Green Bay. From there on I had to drive about 60 plus miles northwest to a small town, where there was a small cookie baking company who was interested making they own plastic cookie trays.

The problem was that the scheduled meeting was set up for Monday morning. That met that I had to travel there Sunday. From California even that I take the earliest flight I will arrive late in the evening. The connecting flight from Chicago to Green Bay was the last flight to go there and it was going to take off at 10 pm. It was a small commuter aircraft. In the meantime one of the biggest snow storm hit Wisconsin. The small airliner keep delaying the takeoff because hopping that the weather will improve. We keep receiving countless delays, but finally the pilot decided to takeoff and fly to Green Bay. The time was close to mid night.

After airborne we encountered very rough weather, bouncing a lot and we never removed the seatbelt. Finally the pilot announced the we approaching the airport and we getting downward for landing. As we getting closer to the ground I was looking out the window, and I saw very heavy snow falling, it looked like a heavy white curtain. The pilot made a remarkable landing, which I don't know how he did it because the snowing was so heavy that could not see anything front of us.

Finally we are in Green Bay after all. As we leaving the airplane the pilot wiped his forehead and said it was not easy, but we made it. That was a heroic effort. After landing I went to the car rental agency to rent a car to go on my way to the small town where were my meeting was the following day.

The rental agent complained that he had to stay that long because the airplane was late and he should be home because the bad weather. Too bad I still had to go about 60 miles from here. After renting the car I studied the map as which way to go, but in the hurry I did not checked what kind of car I have and under the poor lighting I did not checked what color is the car. I was happy that it started in that miserable weather. The weather get rapidly worst and I started to drive. The snow was falling so heavily the wipers almost could not keeping up cleaning the windshield. As I am getting on to the highway which not cleaned. Who cleans the road Sunday after midnight? The road was covered with a heavy snow blanket and the only way I could judge that I was driving on the road that on the side of the road was telephone poles, otherwise I could be driving on some farm land.

The radio in the car constantly saying that nobody should be outside, especially driving in this kind of weather, it is dangerous, and you could lose your life, just stay home. But I am on the road slowly but moving ahead. Finally I came up to a stop sign and that told me that I was on the road up to now. I made a left turn onto the next road and after a short distance I pulled in to the small town, my destination. The hotel was next to the road and I just made it to the parking space, in the front. I just pulled my belongings and entered to the lobby. As I take my suiter out from the car, It became so hard like a cardboard because of the extreme cold temperature. The clerk was also happy to see me and after checking in I was rushing to my room. Lost my energy the only thing I was able to do take a hot shower and go to bed.

The next morning looking out the window the snowing stopped, but everything was covered by a heavy snow blanket. I made my self- ready to go and went outside. My puzzlement was: which is my rented car. First of all I did not remember what was my car's color and make. The rental papers was still in the car the only thing I had is the keys. The only way I could find which my car is to try the key, if it opens it is the correct car. So the only way to find out is to start cleaning the door from the snow and try to fit the key. If the key do not fit it is not my car. I went to the first car than the next and so on, until the key worked, and the meantime all the people looking trough the windows and thinking if I am planning to steal a car or not. Finally the fourth car it was mine.

As I opened the door and turned the ignition on now I was ready to go to work, However the starting of the car activated the wipers which dumped all the snow on to my lap, since the door was still open. Now I had to get out of the car to clean myself from the snow, but a lot of snow went on to the floor of the car. That clump of the snow never melted in the three days of my stay in spite the heater was on all the time.

The lessons of this experience was that I should not gone in the middle of a sever snow storm and jeopardize my life. O well I was young and foolish, ignoring the fact that I could have driven into a ditch and stock there freeze to death, before they find me Monday morning. I had no heavy coat with me, and at that time we had no cellphones. Late Sunday night no body cleans the highways. But the duty to be there and do the job right out ways any fear you have.

Snow storm in Detroit

I was heading to Lancing Michigan for an important meeting. I am going to meet with an automotive supplier executives who's planning to open a manufacturing plant in Canada to make automobile head liners. To get there I had to take a flight from LAX to Detroit. The weather was very warm in Los Angeles, about 82 degree but, in Detroit was very wintery. I decided to pack my suite case with the heavy outfits on the top portions and when I arrive there I will change to the winter clothing at the airport. This way I am not over dressed in LA and I am also comfortable on the airplane. The flight expected to arrive in the late evening hours. I thought I should not accepted to go because of my previous experiences in winter weather traveling, but the meeting was important for future work. When you are consulting you have to go when they ask you other wise they may will obtain someone else and put yourself out of work and earning money. There is no second chance. So I was prepared for another cold and snowy experience.

The flight was ok no deviations from a routine flight. As we approached the Detroit airport and we prepared to land, the airplane almost touched down. I could see the runway from the window then the plane lifted off from the airport, and went into a holding pattern. The pilot came on the telecom and told us that the runway was very icy and heavy side winds did not offered safe landing. It is heavy snow storm in the area and we have to land somewhere else but not in Detroit. A little wile after that he told us that no other airport is open and the only airport is available is Chicago, so we will land there. About circling an hour finally we have landed in Chicago. We have landed safely, but our problem was that no ramp was available to unload because all the Midwestern airports has been closed down and all those flights landed in Chicago, way too many airplanes on the ground. All the airplanes were parked on the taxiway and no open stalls to unload. They also told us that they not going to unload our luggage they will keep it on the airplane since we will continue our flight in the morning This is when my idea backfired, to put the heavy close in the suite case. The outside temperature in Chicago were minus 20 degree.

The airline provided hotel room vouchers and told us that most of the hotel rooms are packed so we may be bussed to the surrounding suburbs we may have too double up with strangers; None of us liked it. With lightly clothed people we boarded the shuttle van outside and told the driver to turn on the heater. He has told us that the heater was on since the morning, but the windows head frosting on the inside. All the people complained about the cold, saying that this is not "a civilized" conditions. We had been shuttled a great distant to a hotel and by the time we got there, the restaurant was closed there for we did not get fed and had to go to bed with an empty stomach. The next morning was a pandemonium at the airport because all the dropped off passengers showed up looking for the flight continue to the original destinations. The weather improved and the flights are eventually moving. In the mean time I have received a call from my wife that the people in Lancing looking for me and they are wondering where I was. One of the executive was on the same flight but he managed to take a train from Chicago to Detroit so he made it to the meeting. I was not aware of that option and any way my luggage was on the airplane..

My wife told them that I was stock in Chicago, but I will be there the next day. Finally we have boarded the plane and ended up in Detroit. I got my luggage and opened it to dress up for the cold weather in my winter outfit, as was planned. I went outside and got a taxi. When I told the driver where I am heading he told me that he can only go so far because the roads are not cleaned yet and he will drop me off at a shopping center. It is not far from my final destination. I telephoned from the shopping center to the company and they told me someone will pick me up and bring me to the meeting. Not very long a fellow showed up in a very light trench coat shivering, I was sorry for him, I guess he was not prepared for this extreme cold condition ether . He has taken me to the offices where our meeting finally occurred. This was an experience I will not forget and I made up my mind that stay away to travel in the winter to the east-coast or the mid-west especially when they predicting extreme weather conditions.

TRIP FROM EL CENTRO TO YUMA

I had to go to Yuma Arizona; I was working on the Iceberg lettuce rapping project. The company I was working with produced the plastic wrapping material. The Yuma area was the winter growing area that is why I had to go there. My flight would take me from LAX to Yuma direct in the evening time after dark. It was a very stormy rainy evening and the weather reports predicted imminent heavy thunder storm activity. The small commuter plane we were scheduled on took off from LAX airport and was heading to Yuma city. As the plane reached flying altitude we had to fly thru very heavy thunder clouds, and it was pitch dark with heavy rain covering the plane. We have experienced major bouncing not only up and down but sideways as well. The thunder activity included bright flashes of lightening and it was all over the sky. As I was looking out the window it was very close to the wings of the plane, we were all scared. The pilot came in the intercom and he has told us that he has difficulty to keep the plane safe and he will touch down at the nearest airport available. He will go to El Centro and land there. Luckily we made it down and all of us were very frightened by the severe thunder activity and for our life. We made it down safely and were happy to be on solid ground.

At the airport the pilot came to us and told us that he was finished flying and because of no improvement in the weather our air journey is ended. The airline company will rent a car for us and we have to go that way to Yuma. He has selected me as the driver. {I think he has chosen me because I looked responsible and reliable to him.} They have rented a limo type large vehicle for all the passengers and they luggage. It was about eight of us, and we all piled into the car. I saddled into to the driver's seat and started out to ward Yuma. The highway was strait and easy. We have moved at the proper speed limit in spite of heavy rain and the wipers barely kept up with it. Above us the thunder storm made a racket, lightning strikes came to the ground, but luckily did not hit us.

Thru the ride no body was talking, everyone did not wanted to say anything. May be all of them were scared of the situation or may be scared of me, that I may not take them to the destination. There were a couple of grand- parents to visit the grand children in Yuma. They did not say anything just kept quiet, but talking could have made the trip more pleasant.

Finally we have reached the state line and we have seen the lights of Yuma city.

With ease we pulled in to the airport and parked at the baggage claim area where worried relatives were waiting for us. Everybody get out of the car, removed they luggage and a few of them thank me for the safe ride.

I turned the limo type car into the rental agency and the same time I rented a small passenger car for my own use. We all went our way probably thinking that this trip concluded safely after all.

ACCIDENTLY ELUDING TSA

We are sanding home our granddaughter from an extended summer vacation with us in California. She is flying alone back to Wisconsin. This is the time when the "Unabomber" scare was in effect. The authorities warned us for delayed boarding time because of the extra scrutiny at check in time. It was recommended that we will need at least two hours extra time for checking in before the departure.

Before all that we had a two hour drive time reaching the airport. So we left early enough to accommodate for everything else. We can't be late because her ticket was a nonrefundable purchase to save money. We have showed up at the ticket counter at the airport where we get her boarding pass and checked her luggage in.

We also learned that we as grandparents we could accompany her directly to the airplane, because she is flying alone. After that we could go upstairs and go true the TSA screening, where all the carryon items will be checked, including our purses and pocket items. All those things placed on the moving belt which traveled true a tunnel for checking. Finally we were true the checking and cleared to go inside the boarding area. We still head extra time before she would boarding the airplane, which she would be one of the first because she is flying unattended. Usually the stewardess come and takes her in to the airplane, and we had to sign some papers. So with the extra waiting time we sat down, just relaxing until boarding would start. She is five years old and done this trips several times before. The flight is none stop flight to Milwaukee and her parents will meet her there.

We just waiting and making some small talk and relaxing. Our granddaughter also had a carryon bag which she packed by herself and inside she had craft work sat a side to have something to do on the airplane it will make the flight time go by faster.

All of the sudden she reached in to her bag and pulls out a large scissor to trim some papers for her craft project. The scissor must have been an eight inches long blade and she started to cut and trim some of her papers with it. I my self was surprised and opened my eyes to see that big scissor. How we get true the security with it and how come it was not spotted and confiscated.

The first thing came to my mine to tell her to put it away in the hurry and don't remove it until home. Just hide it as soon as possible. If anyone seen it we would be in trouble. It did not planned use as a weapon just a mistake and packed in to the carryon luggage by a five year old.

But on the other hand I wandered as how many formidable weapons came and went true undetected and how good is the inspection system we have.

You can't do that!

I was picked up by a college of mine in a rented car and we visited a prospective customer in southern California. I had return airplane tickets to go home after our meeting. The meeting taken a little longer and I was worried that I could miss my flight from Ontario to LAX and the connecting flight to home. The fellow I was with he has insured me that I am not going to miss my plane, we have enough time to get to the airport. As we traveling in the car traffic snarls slowed us down further more. Now I started to really worry and I know that if I miss the flight it would mean a hotel stay for overnight will be coming.

The departure time was very close and we are not even close to the airport, not even seeing at the distance. The partner of mine to gain time started driving crazy.

Finally we are the airport and getting closer, but we are not at the flight checking area yet. He stepped on the gas and started driving crazy. To find a short cuts he has driven the rented car across sidewalks, jumping the curbs several times. Finally we have reached the plane's departure time and I was convinced that it is too late, and we see the small commuter plane started to move away and started to taxi on the taxiway. All of the sudden front of us was an open gate and he drives true it and we are on the taxiway chasing the moving aircraft. I said to him you just can't do this, we can be arrested for driving on the airport grounds .*We was* catching up with the aircraft and pulled on the side of it signaling to stop. To my surprise the pilot just does that and we are side by side, and they opening the door. I just jump out of the car and climbed into the cabin of the airplane. They closed the door and we proceeded to the runway to take off.

I have broken out in a sweat from the rush and breading hard all the way to LAX. All the other passengers looking at me trying to find out who am I and what has happened.

Who can say this can't be done. We just did it!

THE MISS PLACED KEYS

This time I was heading to the east and my flight was a small commuter aircraft taking me to LAX for a connecting flight. The small airplane loaded us up and we were taxiing out to the runway to take off. We had as many passengers, approximately eight or ten of us on the plane.

All of the sudden there was a commotion in the back of the plane. A passenger talked to the stewardess, he has a problem. In the morning he came to the airport with his wife and he was driving the car. At the airport not thinking he put the keys into his pocket. He has discovered just momentarily in the airplane that the keys are in his pocket. Both the car and the house keys together. He knows that his wife will be stranded without the keys. What can be done? In the meantime we are airborne and heading to LAX.

The stewardess went into the cockpit and talked to the pilot. She came back and told the passenger to give her the keys. The pilot will turn around and without landing he will make a low level flite over the runway and drop the keys down on the runway. In the meantime he will radio the authorities at the tower to tell them what is going to happen. They have tied a bright colored paper piece to the keys and when we approached the runway the pilot opened the cockpit window and dropped the keys with the paper onto the runway. As we lifted off we could see that an airport attendant with an electric cart going to pick up the keys. All turned out well without a hitch or regulatory objection.

I don't know if in a similar situation, today, this can be done, but at that time we did it!

WE MADE IT THERE
BUT NOT EXACTLY

I was going to Sacramento for a meeting. The travel agent booked me to fly with a new airline company just came on serving this specific route. The airline company's name was Pioneer Airline. What an appropriate name for an upcoming airline company.

At the airport early in the morning is very busy, because several airline companies scheduled departures. Many people were there to find they appropriate airplanes or flight. I was going around trying to find the ticket counter for this specific airline company. I could not find it, seemed to me that they were so new they did not have opened one yet. As I wonder around I spotted an individual in a dark suite with the Pioneer Airline logo on his jacket. The suite was so wrinkled it looked like he has slept in it. I walked up to him and asked where I should check in and how I will know when we will departure.

He has insured me that everything is on schedule and I will be notified when ready to go. I was just hanging around waiting, all of the sudden somebody whistled at me and signaled that I should follow him. It was the same individual in the wrinkled suite. I followed him out to the tarmac where the airplane was parked. It was an older aircraft, actually a "taildragger" meaning that the tail of the airplane is on the ground. The two bigger wheels are under the wings.

He has ushered me into the plane and actually he was the pilot. Another individual was the copilot. I told him that I did not get my boarding pass yet. He told me that I will get that in Fresno where we will pick up more passengers. I sat right behind the pilot in the first seat.

He has started up the engines with quite a noise. He has turned around and said that by federal aviation rules I should buckle up, than he started out to the runway. In the meantime he has communicated with the tower and when he has received the go head he opened the throttle and with ear piercing noise we started to speed up. I hear him mumbling "come on baby, please lift up". I see the end of the runway coming closer and closer and the plane is not up yet. Just before panic sets in the tail of the plane is up and we started to be airborne. For a while I see the telephone poles on the side go by and we are up but not very much higher. Eventually we are up at crop-dusters altitudes'. A short time we get close to Fresno and ready to land there. At Fresno a ticket agent meet with us and hand me a boarding pass to continue to Sacramento. A few more passengers join us for the remaining flight.

We went into the same scenario as we did before to get airborne and was heading to Sacramento. Finally we land at the Sacramento airport and we taxied to the side. We parked and ready to debark from the small aircraft. I am looking around and I do not see a terminal next to us. I see terminals on the other side of the airport at great distance away. I asked the pilot about that and his answer was: we are not allowed to park on the other side of the airport, that is the reasons we are this side. How am I going to the terminal, someone waiting for me there? The pilot said to me: "look to the left side than to the right side and if you don't see a plane coming just run across". Good luck to us! We managed to do that without any problem.

To go home after the meeting annoyed by this airline service I have managed to hitch a ride on a private aircraft with other passengers who had the same experiences and the same destinations. We shared the cost by splitting the entire fee. It was less hassle and a lot faster.

WE JUST LEFT THE DOORS OPEN

We are heading to the central valley coast of California. A college of mine will pick me up at the airport with his private airplane. He has a small Cessna singe engine airplane and we were going on that. At our destination we rent a car for ground transportation.

We sat the time when we will meet at the airport early afternoon. He flies in from southern California. This is midsummer time and the temperature very hot, about, 108 degree. My wife drove me to the airport, this way I did not have to leave the car parked under the hot sun during our time away from town.

Shure he was at the airport waiting for me. The small aircraft was parked on the side of the airport under the hot sun.

We greeted each other and I said good bye to my wife and was ready to board the plane. This small aircraft usually does not equipped with air-conditioning unit and being parked on the hot sun the inside temperature must be superhot, may be as much as 160 degree. Of course on both sides the doors was open. We climbed into the plane and he was telling me that when we will reach a higher altitude it will be a lot cooler. He also suggested that after buckling up we will leave the doors open. The propeller will force air in to the cab which will make it more bearable. He started the engine and the propeller made it windy, but it was still hot wind. As we taxied out to runway we left the doors fully open as we took off. We started to climb up the air started to be come cooler and cooler and finally became satisfactory. At that point we shut the doors but it was a distance away from the airport. As we flying northward he was telling me that he wants to land in Reedley to meet someone there at the Reedley's airport he made a previous plans.

Shure enough we very quickly came up on the Reedley's ["international"] airport which had nothing but a small runway and an outhouse. We landed there and found nobody waiting for us, so we took off and continued our journey. Since the airport had nothing, all the radio protocol communications was a waist of effort, plus the fuel used to land and takeoff was a waste of money.

At our final destination I called my wife to let her know that we safely arrived. At that time there was no cellphone service, only public phone was available.

She was happy to hear my voice she worried all that time because we could have fallen out of the airplane when we left the doors open. As we took off she was looking up and seen the doors dangling open letting an opportunity to us falling out of the airplane.

No places for lunch

I came from a large chemical company to work at a small privately owned operation. Coming from the large company we had definite privileges which covered all employees. For example we had specified coffee breaks times and lunch schedules. The company provided a large lunch room facility where anybody could purchase food and beverages and consume it. We could bring our own food if we prefer to do that. There were tables and chairs the whole setups. We could seat together as a group and had conversations with each other. We kept time our self to eat and if we stayed over a little longer no one was scolding us . After eating we all went back to work and get involved with our activity.

In the other hand at the small company where most of the employees payed at hourly wage it was different environment. A bell ring signaled a break time and the same was at the end of it. This was a signal to stop or go back to work.

As a junior executive I had broth my own lunch from home and I eat at my desk, not limited to the bell ringing. I did not had to watch the time that closely, however most of the time I spent less time than what had to be scheduled and I was beck to work sooner.

When I was on the factory floor of the manufacturing area often heard the bell signaling the start of the lunch time I had seen that the workers stopped their activities and grabbed the food containers. There were no specific area provided for them to seat, They sat anywhere they could some sat on boxes, some found a space on a nearby bench or even on the floor, others on the edges of the equipment they worked on. Some of the benches were old and broken down, which never was replaced. Most of them never even washed their hands, just started eating. They had the food in their laps, no table was provided at all. I guess they were used to this situation and no one was complaining and that is how they lived day after day.

I just was very sorry for them and I found it unfair to treat workers in such a way. My background experience was different because my previous job, and I just can't treat people that way.

UNCONTROLLED ANGER

The company I had worked for moved into a brand new facilities. The plant was built to a normal factory standards. A large concrete floor and concrete walls, which were poured flat on the top of the floor and stud up right. After securing the walls a roof was placed on the top of it. The office area was attached to the front of the plant with a lower roof configurations. The actual offices portioned into smaller office spaces for the office staff and one corner made into the owner/ general manager. Plenty spaces was set aside for the secretarial staff. Up front was a place for the entrance lobby, where the receptionist sat and operated the telephone switchboard. The back end of the office space where the bathroom facilities was set up with separate lady's and men's rooms. This facility was set for the office personal.

Since this facility was on back side of the offices, to save expanses they have elected to build a factory bathroom. This way common plumbing can be used for both facilities, and share the design features. Actually both were identical; both had the same number of sinks and toilets. The only difference was one had entrances from the office side while the other from the plant side. Everything was brand new when we moved in. All of the facilities were shiny and ready for use, fresh paint and new plumbing, sparking clean, smelled good.

We were proud of our new work place and enjoyed the new factory. We had been in this new plant less than a month, and I was coming back from the plant side to the offices. I needed to use the bathroom facility so for convenience, I went in the plant side restroom.

To my surprise when I entered I found the facility totally destroyed. All the sinks were knocked off the walls, the toilets pushed to their sides broken off the floor, the floor were flooded and the stich was horrendous, smelly staff was floating around.

Of course I could not use the facility and I had to report it to management and used the office side of the bathroom. I wondered who could do this kind of destruction and why? The door is lucked between the offices and the plant after hours, so who ever done this must have done this after hours, possibly at night. If it done at day time the office personal would hear the noise. Someone being very angry and in an extreme rage, who working at the night shift, taking out his frustrations on something nearby. I just don't know if this anger were generated against society or just personal domestic problems made this rage, but either way it was very destructive and not at all civilized manners . On the other hand he has destroyed his own facility and now he has no place to go relief himself. The lady's facility was completely untouched!

PAYCHECK VS WELFARE

This time I had worked for a company who had a plant in downtown LA. The plant occupying a rented building with three floors and we had out gown the building. The three floor arrangement also was difficult, we had to use the elevator to move stuff ether incoming supply or finished goods. The wait time for the elevator caused all kind of material flow problem. The ideal situation would be a level floor plan and definitely larger area to work with.

At that time an offer came from the federal government and it was floating around. The offer was: if a plant will be built at an economically depressed area the government will matches the investment expenses. This sounded very good. Our company contemplated to invest one million dollars and the government will subsidize it with matching dollars. With two million dollars a very nice plant could be built.

The application finalized and the government accepted it, and the building set at the specified location and was built rapidly. We had moved in and started the hireling from the large unemployed pool.

We had reached close to six months at the new plant and the predicament started. The small print of the agreement came in to focus. Based on the agreement with the government we had to hold onto the newly hired employees minimum of six months. The problem was that those employees most of them had very little education and no skills, not very well trainable. That is the reason why they had been unemployed, and entire neighborhood is that way. As time went on, one by one started to leave the company.

The chief engineer came to me with a request that I should talk to those employees, I may have a better communication abilities and convince them to stay in their job. Well I could try but with my job qualification

and compensation level I thought it would be costly for the company that I do a personal manager's job. But a lot more money was at risked therefore I will try my best. Some of the employees I could not talk to because I don't speak Spanish.

There was a fellow named George a middle age man with a family and six kids. His job was to sweep the floors of the plant. He did a fine job of that and he worked hard but he was contemplating to quit his job. We could not upgrade him for a higher position because he had no skills and he could not be trained.

I tried to talk to him and hopping I could convince him to stay on the job at a little longer.

He has sat me strait with his wisdom. To hold his job he had to get up early in the morning and drive to work, and stand 8 hours and push a broom and collect all the dirt, banding over and dumping the waste. When he gets his weekly paycheck, he receives a lot less because of all the deductions versus what he was promised. If he is on welfare all he has to do to drive the welfare office once a week and his welfare check is larger than his take home paycheck. He did not have to work, just stay home and do nothing. His younger wife and six children all was taken care of without any effort.

I guess a job satisfaction and accomplishment is not the driving force, no plans for the future, all was taken care of, by us! My convincing just went out the window.

UNNECESSARY EMBARRASSMENT

I had to go to Carson California for a very important meeting. The driving distance was about 120 miles there. I started out very early in the morning to be there by 10am. The meeting was with a large company's executives, some of them traveled from the east coast for this meeting.

As I was driving, I enjoyed the good weather and the beautiful scenery of the mountains on the side of the road.

Feeling good and looking forward to this meeting and see all this executives whom I talk to but never meth in person.

I know that they are also looking forward to hear the outcome of the project I was involved with, which was most Important for future manufacturing plans for their factory.

As I was getting closer to my destination, about 20 miles short the generator indicator light came on. The light didn't come fully on just flickering, but indicating that there is a problem in the electrical charging system. I know that this problem would not immediately shut down the engine but eventually will happen. The car is running on the battery's power supply. So I did not stopped on the freeway but continued to my destination. With the flickering indicator light I pulled into company's parking lot and parked the car. Just in case after shutting down I tried to start it again and it started up. I had no more time to thinker because the scheduled meeting was ready to start. I went into the office and told the receptionist that I had experienced car problems and she should get a hold of the nearby dealer and they should pick the car up and take it to their service department. The car will start and drivable I will be in a meeting and they should call me when they found the problem. I was confident that she will take care of my request. The next thing I went into the meeting where all of the six executives waiting for me seating at a round conference table. As the meeting went on we discussed many things and I tried to answer questions they had. Notes were made and the discussion went on.

All of the sudden the receptionist came in to the meeting room with a telephone in her hand and placed it on the middle of the conference table. She told me that the call is for me from the service department of the car dealer. They are on the line wanted to talk to me. First of all I was embarrassed the telephone call interrupted our meeting, secondly I did not wanted all of us hear the discussion between me and the dealer. Everyone will hear the predicament I had with my car. So I answered the call, and talked to the service manager. He has informed me that I have a big problem with my car: I need a new generator, a new voltage regulator and a new battery, which would cost me with the installation fee close to $800.00 dollars.

All the executives hear this and looking at me as what I will do. I don't have that kind of money on me and I do not whish to spend so much. I told the service manager: do not replace anything, just charge up the battery and I will pay for that and the original diagnosis cost, thank you; I will pick up the car that evening. The service manager asked me how far I am planning to go? I told him that about 150 miles, he sad you would not make it. And with it we finessed our conversation.

All the executives looking at me and thinking what a brave decision I just made. At the end of the meeting all six of them took me to the dealer to pick up my car and all of them whished me luck. Some of them mentioned that if it would be them reluctantly would pay for the service. I got home safely and removed the generator and took it to a service place and $52.00 spending it was fixed, The battery and the voltage regulator need not be changed and two years later I traded the car in with both questionable equipment.. Lather some of the executives stated that they have learned from me to be more gutsy in the future. I learned that no needed to be embarrassed!

A CHAINSAW INCIDENT

Chainsaws are important tools to handle tree or bush trimmings. Curtain care has to be done when handling such tools because imminent danger exist when it is running. There are sharp moving parts which capable to cut not only skin but limb as well. I know it very well I happen to own one of these types of tools. At this time we are {I myself, my wife and our son} traveling to Burbank California by car. We are on the freeway and we are almost there. The next exit would come up soon where we will exit the freeway. I noticed by the signs that maintenance work is done on the side of the freeway. They are working on the landscape area. We are already on the right lane contemplating the upcoming exit.

All of the sudden a CALTRAN pickup truck starts up from the side and rapidly accelerating to our lane to gain freeway speed. The tailgate of the truck is open and on the truck bed there are some equipment stored. The truck hit a bump and spilling the equipment on to the roadway. Among the equipment spilled there are three or more chainsaws. The chainsaws are rather large, about 18" saw blades. When they hit the road surface, they not only slipping, but violently spinning around. Two or three of the chainsaws spanned in to the left lanes while one of them ended up right front of us, still spinning. I could not avoid it, but I wanted to hit it in the middle of our car.

If the chainsaw ends up under our front wheel at the high speed we moving could cause us to flip over. I managed to do that without much deviation from our designated lane. In the mean time I heard crunching and heavy scraping from the undercarriage of our car coupled with crunching and tire squealing from the left of us. The chainsaw stuck under our car and since it is a very low clearance car it is firmly stuck there made a screeching sound. I was aware that the chainsaw and the road surface creates a large amount of sparks and I also thinking that the gasoline tank of the chainsaw rupturing definitely will ignite and cause a fire.

Luckily our exit point was right there and I pulled out on that and immediately parked there. After stopping I get out and looked under neat. Luckily there was no fire, I guess by moving the gas spill did not get the ignition, the spill was behind us. I tried to dislodge the chainsaw but it would not budge. I get back to the car and moved it a little backward. Still did not want to come out. One more time I moved a little more backward and at this time I managed to move the chainsaw. Of course I had to do this by lying on the dirty ground, by luck and several try I managed to remove the mangled chainsaw out.

The unit showed a complete destructions and useless condition, I just left it on the side for the CALTRAN workers to clean it up or may use it to request a replacement from our tax money.

I wandered if any damage was made to our car, but it was running good and I did not see any fluid leakage there for considered that we were very lucky, did not flipped over or burned down just because a carless worker did not close the tailgate before driving.

FOREIGN FRUIT

I was visiting Ventura California at the strawberry fields. This is early spring and the harvesting of strawberries was going on. Strawberries practically growing year around in Southern California, however the early harvest fetch the highest price especially in the East Coast or Europe because they are still in the winter mode.

I was involved designing a clear plastic container for strawberries which would replace the wood or the flimsy green ribbed plastic baskets.

At the strawberry field I was talking with the foreman of the fruit picking crew and admiring the large stack of strawberry boxes ready to be ship. The strawberries looked gorges, large and plump very shiny. It was very appetizingly outstanding.

He was telling me that this shipment was heading to Europe, actually to London England. That afternoon will be taken to Los Angeles and loaded on to an airplane heading to London overnight.

As we talking we have chucked in our discussion that the strawberries will arrive in London the next morning and will be distributed. And furthermore we talked about the scenario that any of the Californian tourists headed to London via the same airplane. They are seating in the cabin while the strawberries in the belle of the aircraft.

After they arrival the next morning at the restaurant ordering fresh strawberries, thinking that this fruit grown in England and could saying they sure know how to grow so delicious berries in here.

But after all it made the same trip as they did. They may have been fantastically surprised or perhaps fooled.

I WANTED TO GO HOME

I was in Dallas Texas ready to board a connecting flight. I came in with a other plane from the east coast and I was ready to continue to go home. The travel agency booked me on that specific flight because of substantially reduced fare and by changing planes the ticket was much less.

The flight I was scheduled to continue my trip was going from Dallas via Denver where we will stop and continue to Bakersfield. Up to now everything went well right on schedule.

The airline company at the boarding area called us to be ready to board the aircraft, and we all saddled in our assigned seats. We were ready to go and fly.

At that time an announcement came on the intercom that we will not be ready to move yet, because they had received notifications that the Denver did not had so favorable weather conditions and we should delay our departure.

The first half hour went by, than another half hour, than after an hour a second announcement came in, that the Denver airport is really sucked in with strong wintery weather conditions and we have to wait longer. I know that Denver is a problem in the winter time and airport closing often happen.

An idea popped in to my head, that there is another flight to Bakersfield by another airline, which frequently I took, and its departure time is scheduled in about 40 minutes. If I stay here and Denver's condition did not improve I not only miss the other plane but I may stock overnight at the airport or may end up in a hotel stay.

I went up front and asked for my boarding pass back and will run to the other airline and board it. The stewardess complied with my request and found my boarding pass among the large stack of boarding passes and handed back to me.

Now I had to hustle to the other terminal and try to locate the proper boarding area for the direct flight to Bakersfield. Running fast I made it and close to the time when they closing the door.

I was talking to the stewardess to accept my boarding pass from another airline company. She said to me that she can't do that, she needs her supervisor approval. She had to call downstairs. She came back and told me that I have to pay an extra $100.00 top on my boarding pass.

I don't want to do that and I know I had to use my best salesmanship effort to remedy the situations.

I told the stewardess let me talk to the supervisor ether by phone or in person.

The supervisor came upstairs and we could talk.

I told him that if they have an open seat and they take off as is, they not going to gain anything more than what they already collected. An open seat does not generate any income, but if he takes my existing boarding pass is extra money. If the flight is already in the red, it will minimize the loss. Is that makes any since?

He was thinking for a moment and saw it my way and agreed with me.

Accepted my boarding pass and I was on the plane.

Good and fast thinking got me home and on time.

Forklift meets the freeway

This incident was told me by a good friend of mine. He had given me the permission to write up this incident. The company he had worked for transferring an electric forklift from the plant to a sister facilities of theirs.

The two workers who going to do that backed up with the truck to the loading dock and drove the forklift on to the truck bed. They secured it with chains so it cannot move. Closed the tailgate and got ready to drive off.

Both guys saddled in the cab and with a big smile that the job was done, started to drive off. The route takes them on the regular streets and further on the freeway.

Speeding toward they destination they had hit some bumps which jarred everything on board. Some of the bumps were little while some was really big.

The smile still on they face just feeling good rushing forward all of the sudden an underpass came front of them on the freeway.

When they placed the forklift on the truck they forget to turn off the main electric power switch. The constant jarring motion activated the forklift's elevating actuator and forks started to move upwards. By the time they had reached the underpass the forks was fully extended to maximum height. The upcoming underpass clearance was less than the extended forks height plus the truck bed height

So with a huge bang when the two met it knocked the forklift off the truck's bed, damaging and tearing the tie -down chains, and truck's bed with it. The forklift ended on its side on the road surface also badly damaged.

The pervious smiles disappeared from the fellows faces.

The job was incomplete and mistake was its consequences.

Wrong first impression

I was telephoning a prospective client and when they answered my call always his secretary did that. It was the most pleasant voice, like a little angel talking. She had a very cheerful and a sexy way to talk. Matter-of- fact to me it was so sexy that I was looking forward to meet this woman.

Several months passed and finally I had an opportunity to visit that company. As I said earlier I was really looking forward meet this sexy girl.

As I walked in a lady was at the front receptionist post and I introduced myself, and the same time I was glancing around to locate the particular sexy lady I got to know via the telephone conversations.

She jumped up and introduced herself that she is the one I was talking with in the past.

It was a total surprise; she was not the sexy lady I pictured before. That was just an illusions I created myself. She was not bad looking, but a lot shorter and heavier than I pictured in my mine, only her voice was the same and most sexy and alluring.

At a different time I visited another company. The receptionist at the front was a good looking young lady. I liked her and I know that she was pregnant. After a while in a couple weeks she no longer was at work. I asked where she was and I was told that she had a baby.

Time went by and when I was back again at that company she was at the front again. Behind her desk was a small bassinet covered with a baby blanket. I was happy to see that and I know that there was a baby in it. So I politely ask if I could see the baby. She said OK and I proceeded to lift the blanket away so I can look into the bassinet.

Wahoo!

I saw a little chimps looking back at me. The baby had her eyes to close to each other, was reddish, full of wrinkles on the face and it appeared to me she had some facial hair also. First I could not say anything, than I said ok well she is a life. Than I was thinking that this woman must have a very ugly husband who may looks like a monkey.

When I went home and told this incident to my wife she immediately told me that baby must be premature baby and will look good later on. She knows she had worked with premature babes.

After several weeks later I asked the mother if the baby was born prematurely and she told me that she was premature. And that time the baby looked good.

Now on I guess one more clue can be added that, according to Darwin we human beings involved from apes long time ago.

CRICKET INVASION

I went to Iowa to work with a meat processor who is introducing a microwaveable dish. The plastic dish contains a stew like meal and when it is warmed in a microwave oven it will be consumed. The criteria were to see if the plastic dish will take the heat without distorting and make it unusable. This product line will be the first for this company. We were going to do some test runs to find out which plastic container will do the job.

The day before I have going to the plant I checked in to the local Motel, which is the only one near the plant. At checking in the front desk they informed me that all the front rooms are under construction and the only thing is available is in the back side of the building. It is alright for me the only reason I will use the room is take a quick shower and sleeping. I will be away working the rest of the time.

I checked in and went to my room and since it was evening time, I showered to wash off all the travel dirt and climbed in to bed. As soon as I turned out the lights, hearable noise level covered my room. What is this noise? I turn on the lights and the noise stops. Turn the light off and a few seconds later the noise is back. I repeat the switching of the light with the same results.

It just downed to me the noise coming from crickets in my room, not just one but many of them and all want out do each other. It is they mating rituals and all of them in my room. Of course they came in from the corn field back of the Motel. The big corn field and the Motel's back only a narrow sidewalk separate and they have crawled in under the door.

Now I had to find them and hopefully get rid of them. I did not see any of them openly they hiding behind somewhere in the room. When the light is on they keep quiet, when the light is off I can't see them. I started investigating with the light on and lifting the pictures away from the wall. There I found three or four behind the picture and smash them to dead. All the pictures had about the same numbers of bugs. I killed them all, but by the time I finished the killing field daytime started to creep in to the room.

Now it is quiet, but I had to get up and go to work, with the remaining sounds of the cricket noise in my head.

I am positive that the next tenant in this Motel will have the same experience.

I HEARD AND I UNDERSTOOD

I wanted to finish my story telling with one of the funniest situation I have encountered.

I had worked in the central coast of California area and after finishing there I was heading home via airlines.

My flight was going from Monterey via San Francisco and from there on.

I had just boarded a small commuter aircraft at the Monterey airport in late afternoon times. Several passengers were ready to board including myself. We had seat assignments and we boarded accordingly, first starting from the back of the plane. My scheduled seat was in the middle section of the plane. Other people came on board after me, and two very attractive women came on board right after me and saddled right front of me. I had no one next to me.

As the plane started to move and get ready to take off the noise was loud enough to talk or hear anything. But after a while the noise diminished and people stated to talk. The two ladies engaged in conversations with each other. The noise level still was high enough that they started talking a little louder. Matter- of- fact it got loud enough that I could hear them very well.

Than recognized that they are talking in my native language which I have mastered from childhood on.

The conversation covered in full detail of the sexual encounters in the resort of Monterey. They talked about

the different fellows and what they did with them.

At first taught I should stop it. Oh well it is entertainment, so I did not interfered.

I did not know that ladies talk so openly about this kind of subjects, on the other hand to my knowledge man does.

They had no fear thinking who would understand the language at these occasions; they did not curtail the discussions in full details, who would understand it?

I my self-seating in the back of them alone I can hear everything they saying.

As we landed in San Francisco and started to deplane I cut up with the two woman and wished a pleasant day in they own language. I don't know that they turned white or red, but I am sure they were ready to sink in to the ground.

Oops

I hope I managed to list all the incidents from my memory bank. Oops……..

In case I will remember one more I could listed here, but it is too late the book is finished!

PS My foot note to the travels I have made in the past. .It is remarkable that I have covered such a great distances to earn my leaving. In the not so past most individuals earned they leaving near their homes. Many jobs were chosen where people leaved. I made my work area not near but all over the US and Canada. Each place I worked and earned money, at the airports I purchased in the gift shops a "momentum spoon" removed the emblem from the handle and reattached it to my pen box top, this way I remember where I have traveled and earned my leaving. The pen box is loaded with the emblems. It has been a privilege and some LUCK.

Grateful to God to let me earn the living in that fashion, and without any major accident, just a few mishaps.